BY THE SAME AUTHOR

*In This Name: The Doctrine of the Trinity
in Contemporary Theology*

*Protestant Christianity: Interpreted
Through Its Development*

(with John Dillenberger)

THE REALITY
OF THE CHURCH

The Reality

of

THE CHURCH

by

Claude Welch

CHARLES SCRIBNER'S SONS

New York

TO
ERIC, THOMAS, CLAUDIA

PREFACE

IN WRITING the following chapters, I have been guided by two general delimiting principles, one involving form and the other substance. The form of the presentation has been partly governed by the fact that the material was prepared for delivery as the James Sprunt Lectures at Union Theological Seminary, Richmond, Virginia, in February 1958. Although the argument is here offered in much greater length than could be encompassed in a course of six lectures, it has seemed best to retain the pattern of a straightforward, constructive statement in the text. Explicit and extended reference to other contemporary literature has been kept to a minimum, and placed almost entirely in notes.

In content, this book is conceived as an essay on the ontology of the church. It is simply an attempt to define the reality of the church, to answer the question: wherein does the church have its *being?* Where it has been necessary to venture into related problems, I have done so only in so far as this might contribute to the central theme. Thus, for example, the Christological statement in Chapter III is not proposed as a complete doctrine of Incarnation, but only of certain fundamental features thereof. Similarly, several items which would call for extended treatment in a full doctrine of the church—*e.g.*, sacraments, ministry, church discipline—are here only briefly discussed. I have intended rather to develop a perspective in which these and related problems may properly be viewed.

One of the central themes in this analysis is that suggested for study by the Lund Conference (1952), the relation of the church to Christ and the Holy Spirit. But the development of this motif, I am convinced, must be set in the context of the wide variety of ways in which the New Testament describes the church; and though I have not attempted to deal explicitly with all the New Testament images, I have sought to be faithful to that variety. Furthermore, an adequate statement of the dialectic of Christ and the church must take seriously several elements which have tended to be partially obscured in contemporary interest in the "Christological foundation" of the church. These include, especially, the real humanity of the church, the sin of the church, and the importance of eschatology for the church. Only as these are properly recognized can we speak of the church in the wholeness of its relation to the Triune God.

To the faculty and trustees of Union Theological Seminary in Richmond, I want to express my deep gratitude for the honor of being invited to deliver the Sprunt Lectures and for their hospitality and kindness during the week I spent in Richmond. I am greatly indebted also to my colleagues in the North American and European sections of the Theological Commission on Christ and the Church. My argument in this book has been formulated in the context of the discussions of these groups during the past four years, and I hope that it may prove a contribution to the further study of the church in the ecumenical movement. Finally, my thanks go to several colleagues at Yale, who have read part or all of the manuscript and have made most helpful suggestions, Professors Hans W. Frei, James M. Gustafson, George A. Lindbeck, and Paul S. Minear.

CLAUDE WELCH

The Divinity School
Yale University
August 1958

TABLE OF CONTENTS

13

THE REALITY
OF THE CHURCH

Chapter 1

THE ENIGMA OF THE CHURCH

I. DIMENSIONS OF THE PROBLEM

WHENEVER the reflective Christian views the church, he finds himself in the midst of disturbing contradictions. If he seeks to discern the one body of Christ amid the multiple societies of the world, he beholds the company of those who call themselves Christian divided into a great variety of "bodies," often ranged over against each other, separated or even estranged from one another, and chiding each other for misunderstanding the will and purpose of the One whom they all claim as their Lord. If he would attend to the "realm of redemption," the sphere of reconciliation of man to God and man to man, in which there is no longer Jew nor Greek, male nor female, slave nor free, his eye is affronted by the familiar patterns of social stratification, by often intensified distinctions of caste and class, and by peculiarly ecclesiastical and religious forms of divisiveness. Where the catholicity of the church, as it relates to the inclusion of all conditions and sorts of men, does come to apparent expression, it is often correlated with the absence of genuinely personal relations among the participants. And where there is intensity of togetherness, warmth of companionship and a sense of belonging with others and to others, this is frequently bought at the price of selectivity and exclusiveness, the bonds of community being formed from commonalities of social, economic, racial or cultural interests; inner cohesion is achieved by the all but verbal jettisoning of the church's claim to inclusiveness.

The life of the church, moreover, whether in particular congregations or in so-called "communions," shows fealty being rendered to many lords. (To no one is this more brutally clear than to the young minister who comes to his first congregation full of zeal as an ambassador of Christ, who will preach Christ crucified and him only, who will be a servant in a community of servants, ministering to and transforming the life of individual and society. He is quickly met by quite different orders of expectation and reality, both in the congregation and in the ecclesiastical hierarchy—and woe be to him if he does not quickly make his peace with them.) Confusion of loyalties distorts in nearly every conceivable way that character of being "in the world yet not of it," which is supposed to be distinctive of the church. In witness and in life, the community is now so isolated from the world in which it exists as to be irrelevant to its needs and forms, now so accommodated to that world as to be only the reflection and defender of the socially accepted values, now simply troubled and uncertain. The spirit which animates the community, and is expressed in its worship, its preaching, its missions, its education, its response to social problems, is often more readily identified with the natural drives, rigidities and imperialisms of institutional power structures than with the Spirit and mind of Jesus Christ. The lives of the members reveal less the joyful song of the "new man" than the tiresome and familiar refrain of the old captivity in which nothing has been made new. The unbeliever can hardly be blamed if he does not perceive in the voice and life of the church that higher freedom, that healing grace, that new unity, that redeeming Word and life in Christ of which the gospel speaks; for the reflective Christian must also wonder at the contradiction between the unity, catholicity, apostolicity and holiness which the creed proclaims and the disunity, partiality, discontinuity and sin which the church embodies, between the new and redeemed humanity so glowingly depicted in scripture and the actual spectacle of mankind which the church presents.

One could continue this sort of description for a long time with vivid documentation from the life of the parish church, or the contemporary scene of Christendom, or the history of Christianity, and there are occasions when such a pursuit would be necessary and salutary, especially for the humbling of our spirits. Yet for the present it is more needful to say that these random comments direct attention primarily to only one side of the problem—namely, to the familiar fact of *sin* in the church. To say that this is only one facet of the matter is not to suggest for a moment that it is insignificant, or, because familiar, no longer in need of fresh theological examination. On the contrary, this is a matter of the greatest import to which we shall have to turn again and again in the course of these chapters; for while the existence of imperfection in the church in history is obvious, the meaning of this, the theological interpretation, is difficult to state.

Nevertheless, as the Christian reflects on the church, he finds this "contradiction" bound up with another sort of puzzle. He has read the sociologists, and he remarks how the church appears, not as a divinely established and ordered commonwealth of men whose citizenship is in heaven, but rather as a quite earthly and human community and institution. Like other religious institutions, the church appears as the fulfiller of certain human drives and desires. It can be studied like other communities of almost every sort. The conditions of unity in the church are seen as the conditions of every social unity, whose members recognize common interests and norms. The church shares in the necessity of every community to express its commonality in certain organs and definite forms. Like the nation, the party, the club and the school, the church has its symbols—whether the repetition of dramatic acts, or the explicit statement of common beliefs, purposes and patterns of behavior—through which the meaning, spirit and interests of the community are transmitted from person to person and from generation to generation. Its authoritative documents can be likened to the scriptures of other institutions, serving as touchstones and norms, as objects of constant reinterpretation and reappropriation, and as vehicles of communication for the root judgments and expectations of the group. The authority of scripture in the church permits comparison with the role of the Constitution in American life, or the common law in Britain, as well as with the Koran in Islam or the Vedas in Hinduism.

Patterns of organization and leadership in the church reveal themselves to be familiar human forms. The ordering of the church may be hierarchical or equalitarian, constitutional or autocratic, bureaucratic or democratic. Authority in the church may depend upon "personal charisma," or unwritten tradition, or it may be assigned and transmitted according to explicitly formulated rules and regulations setting forth conditions of eligibility, selection, functions, privileges and prerogatives. The church even seems to participate in a general pattern of social development, both in its beginning and in subsequent internal movements—a transition from the assembling of followers around a charismatic leader, through the assumption of leadership by the original followers, to increasingly formalized and official authority.

Again, it would be easy to expand this account, but the point will now be at least visible. The church is not exempt from the sort of sociological scrutiny which is applied to every other social group, community or institution. The symbols, practices, structures and documents of the church do not seem to possess any unique resistance to this sort of analysis. On the contrary, the church appears very much a part of the general pattern of human communities, and can readily be taken for simply one of many such communities.

If this be true, then we have to deal with a second sort

of "contradiction" or "paradox" in the life of the church.[1] We can have no sympathy with those who would seek to shelter the church from the analysis of the sociologist as if somehow its forms were too sacred to be touched by the profane hands of science. That is both a counsel of despair and a basic theological error, as we shall see. Our task is not to deny the human character of the Christian community, as here exemplified, but to seek to understand. Nor can we treat these matters as irrelevant to a proper "theological" judgment about the church. Neither can we simply identify this aspect of the problem with the former, for here are "social factors" which raise the question of the nature of the church in a different form from that posed by the presence of sin in the church. (Thus one must beware of the tendency to speak of "social factors" as if the presence of these in the life of the church were a mark simply of failure, and therefore to be negatively evaluated.)

In short, an ambiguity which is at least two-fold strikes the eye of the reflective Christian as he tries to understand the nature of this community of which he is a part. The question of the paradox or contradiction between what

[1] In this chapter, the terms "paradox," "contradiction," "ambiguity," "mystery," "duality," "polarity" and "dialectic," are deliberately used loosely and often interchangeably, in an attempt to suggest the variety of ways in which the problem may be and has been described and to avoid prejudging issues which are the concern of the entire argument. It will be clear from subsequent discussion that these terms are by no means equally appropriate. For the nature of the church as at once historical community and people called of God (see ch. II), I should prefer the term "polarity," while for the nature of the church as at once sinful and holy (see ch. IV), the term "mystery" seems to me most appropriate.

faith asserts about the church and what is evident to the unprejudiced eye, means (1) how can this divided, faltering, sinful company be rightfully called a new creation, the bride cleansed, the community of the justified, the way of salvation, the first-fruits of the new age, the temple of the *Holy* Spirit? (2) How can this association of men, conformable apparently to the patterns of a multitude of other human associations, be rightfully described as the people *of God*, the colony *of heaven*, the *royal* priesthood, *God's* planting, the body *of Christ?*

With this double polarity, our thinking about the church must be concerned throughout. Certainly this is no novel or local problem. Every sector of Christendom has to deal with it—whether Roman Catholic or Orthodox or Protestant, whether "churchly" or "sectarian," whether "liberal" or "conservative." It is a question often decisive for divisions within the church, yet often cutting across formal divisions. It relates to the existence of the parish quite as much as to the universal church. It is as old as the people of Israel. It is no more a question for the modern Christian than for those in Corinth to whom the Apostle wrote— was that not a miserable community indeed, which St. Paul addressed as the "church of God . . . those consecrated in Christ," and described as the temple of God and the body of Christ? And it is a question which has evoked a variety of answers, some of which will be noted in a moment.

Moreover, this double duality of the church is no isolated problem. Apart from the well-known fact that every theological problem seems ultimately to involve every other, this question leads immediately in the direction of at least two similar problems.

1) On the one side, we observe the similarity between the situation of the church and that of the individual Christian believer. The idea of paradox or contradiction in the Christian life is now almost a commonplace of theological literature. We speak familiarly of the "paradox of grace," of being both "in Christ and expecting Christ" or of "having and not yet having," of the hiddenness of our life in Christ, of the conflict of flesh and Spirit. This tension is expressed in the New Testament and is very much a part of Christian experience. It is no longer we who live, Christ lives in us; yet we live in the flesh by faith. We are sinners who must daily confess our sin, yet we are already redeemed in Christ. The Spirit is given to us and the love of God poured into our hearts, yet we live in the flesh and love not. We are sons of God yet groan inwardly waiting for our adoption. And if we are more than conquerors through Christ, the victory is not readily apparent to the bystander. The believer has neither outward halo nor unmistakable divine influence radiating from himself, which must necessarily be convincing to the observer. The Christian is not obviously or self-evidently different from other men. At the least, in Luther's words, "our good is hidden, and that so deeply that it is hidden under its contrary. Thus our life is hidden under death, our joy under hatred, glory under shame, salvation under perdition, heaven under hell, wisdom under foolishness, righteousness under sin, strength

under infirmity." [2] Of course there may be visible, even spectacular changes in the manner of our living as we come to be in Christ. The miraculous work of grace can bring signs visible even to the outsider, and the Christian man can find new and powerful loves within himself. But these manifestations are never wholly unambiguous, certainly to the spectator and perhaps even to the believer himself. The Christian life is therefore both a constant struggle and a problem for faith.

To point to this tension is by no means to be done with it. That must be said because the impression is sometimes given that the mere statement of the duality or contradiction is a sufficient result of theological investigation— which, in my judgment, it is not. To be sure, a genuine recognition of the paradox, if this be the proper term for it, is a notable advance over any kind of evasion, whether through the naive assertion that the Christian is already translated out of struggle into perfection, or through a simple progressivism which transposes victory entirely to the end and denies that redemption is accomplished. Nevertheless, simple acknowledgment of the persistent paradox cannot be the end of theological effort. We must explore its dimensions as precisely as possible and seek to understand what kind of paradox or ambiguity or duality or mystery we are dealing with. And just this effort may both help us in, and be helped by, our attempt to understand the dualities we see in the being of the church.

[2] Weimar Aufgabe. 56.392.28. Quoted in Gordon Rupp, *The Righteousness of God* (London, Hodder and Stoughton, 1953), p. 190.

2) On the other hand, if the problem of the church re-
minds us of the existence of the believer, it also calls to
mind the person of Jesus Christ. In him also we meet an
enigma, as is well shown by the variety of reactions to him
which the New Testament records. By his contemporaries,
Jesus was confessed to be the Son of God, and he was re-
jected as only the son of Joseph the carpenter. He was
variously viewed as a curiosity, as one possessed by demons, as a teacher of wisdom, as a wonder-working healer,
and as a political insurgent. He was followed, and he was
ignored. He was hailed, and he was crucified. From first
to last there is a mystery about Jesus. It is present in his
words (particularly in his words about himself) and in his
deeds. To some these are testimony, to some they are not.
The same is true of crucifixion and resurrection. The New
Testament makes it entirely clear that Jesus could be, and
was, mistaken for any one of a variety of ordinary or
extraordinary human beings. There was (and there is) *no*
externally compelling evidence of divine glory. Every
claim by him or for him, everything in the way of a proof,
appears as ambiguous and problematical, both for Jesus'
chronological contemporaries and for us. Certainly this is
true of miracles, which were attributed also to others and
are nowhere presented in the gospels as adequate to compel assent. While they may be revelation to those who believe, or even the occasion of belief, to others they mean
little or nothing. And if the miracles (the Christological
proofs of an earlier generation) are no exception to the
ambiguity and paradox of Jesus' career, neither are the

"moral excellence" of his life nor the "superiority" of his teaching (the Christological proofs of a more recent generation). And, we may add, neither does the presence of "paradox" serve as a convincing demonstration, though there may be some today who seem to believe this.

Once again, we have before us what appears to be a commonplace in contemporary theology (at least in "post-liberal" Protestant theology)—or, better said, a more or less agreed judgment which permeates the deep concern with Christology in our time and marks one of its great gains. Christology must deal explicitly with the problematic or paradoxical character of all testimony to Jesus Christ. Jesus is not self-evidently the Christ.

In view of this, we may well be disposed to consider the dualities of the church in connection not only with the life of the individual believer, but also and particularly with the person of Jesus Christ. This latter theme comes to us at the moment with especially high recommendations, notably from the now well-known discussions within the World Council of Churches. Our search for unity in the church, or rather our effort to manifest the given unity of the church, will be furthered most, it is suggested, if we turn our attention specifically to Jesus Christ as the head and unity of the church. "The way to Christ is the way to unity!" This is the watchword. The method of comparative ecclesiology, of setting doctrines of the church alongside each other to see more clearly the areas of difference and agreement, has its place, and a meaningful one, but it is essentially limited. Its role is descriptive rather

than creative. It enables us to see more or less clearly where
we stand in relation to each other, but it is not really a
means of advance. Thus at the Lund Conference in 1952
the already famous decision was made to turn to a study of
"the doctrine of the church in close relation both to the
doctrine of Christ and to the doctrine of the Holy Spirit." [3]
That is, instead of viewing the church as it were "in itself," we should try to see the church in relation to its
head and source. In him we may be brought closer together.

The wisdom of such a procedure may find confirma-
tion from several directions. It is significant, for example,
that in the Apostles' and Niceno-Constantinopolitan creeds
the church appears not "alone" but in the context of faith
in the Holy Spirit (and necessarily also in the Father and
the Son). Indeed, it may be argued that here faith is not
confessed in the church as such, not "in itself," but only
in relation to the triune God, who alone can be the object
of faith in the proper sense of the word (see below, ch. II).
Moreover, it appears that what binds together the pro-
fusion of New Testament images referring to the church
is not the presence of one all-embracing master image, providing the principle of unity, but rather the pervasive reference of them all to the person and work of Christ (and
inseparably of the Father and the Spirit). This is a point
which must be explored in greater detail, but for the moment it need only be asserted that Christ (and the Holy

[3] *Report*, p. 11, of the Third World Conference on Faith and Order, held
at Lund, August, 1952.

Spirit) and the church belong together. There is no gospel of Jesus Christ which does not include the church, and certainly no notion of a church which does not center in Christ. Bishop Nygren puts it succinctly, though in a way which needs careful explanation: "The Church cannot exist without Christ; Christ cannot be present without his Church. The Messianic people cannot exist without the Messiah; the Messiah cannot be a Messiah without a people. Thus they are mutually connected one with the other, and this reciprocity is essential. Christology and ecclesiology condition one another." [4]

At the same time, certain dangers are present in the suggestion that we consider together the doctrines of Christ and the church, and if we do not attend to these, we shall be in serious difficulty.

(a) It is certainly ultimately true that "the way to Christ is the way to unity," for only in Christ do we have our unity. But it does not necessarily follow that the way to unity is through the *doctrine* of Christ. Though Christ, the living Lord of the church, can never be divisive, *Christology* can be at least as divisive as ecclesiology —and it may be much more so, because we come closer to the center and object of our faith. The consideration of Christology may be the only possible way, because the true way, to an understanding of the unity of the church, but it may also lead to more radical cleavage. Or, to speak more precisely, since differences in ecclesiol-

[4] Anders Nygren, *Christ and His Church* (Philadelphia, Westminster Press, 1956), p. 31.

ogy may turn out to be rooted in (or corollaries of) differences in Christology, the endeavor may disclose the full depth of the cleavages which actually exist.

(b) It would be an illusion to suppose that we could move by any merely deductive process from an already complete and clearly established doctrine of Christ to a theology of the church. Our apprehension of Christ is not as firmly fixed as all that. To be sure, we do have conciliar decisions respecting the doctrine of the incarnation. And this is significant. Certain guides and limits have been staked out, which must not be ignored. But to assume that we can simply rest there in our Christological toil is absurd. If we must struggle to understand the church in relation to Christ, we must also continually ask anew after the meaning of the person and work of Christ.

(c) Even if this difficulty were not with us, we should still have to beware of any simple correlation (and especially "parallel") of doctrines of Christ and of the church. The church is not Christ, or another Christ; it is not the incarnation. The doctrine of the two natures cannot be directly transferred to the church.[5] Nor can the church be considered exclusively in relation to Christ. It must be viewed also in the context of the work of the Holy Spirit, or, more properly, of the triune God.[6] And the church must be looked at in the light of the situation of the individual believer. (These perspectives are not, of course,

[5] See below, esp. chs. III and IV.
[6] Cf. the well-stated warning in E. Schlink, "Christus und die Kirche," *Kerygma und Dogma*, I, 3 (July, 1955), pp. 208f.

mutually exclusive, nor merely supplementary; they are interrelated and indispensable to one another.)

In view of the factors just mentioned, it seems useful to approach this whole doctrinal complex in terms of the tensions sketched at the beginning of this chapter. Here is a common thread which runs inevitably through our thinking. The paradox of the church directs attention both to the problem of Christ and to the problem of the Christian, though not in precisely the same way. And an examination of various understandings of the church may well show that crucial differences here depend precisely upon whether primary weight is given to the relation between the being of the community and the life of the individual Christian, or to the analogy between the church and Christ. It may be suggested, for example, that in those instances where chief emphasis is laid upon the fragility of the church, its sin, and the lordship of Christ over the church, the controlling thought is the parallel between the being of the church and the life of the believer. On the other hand, where the analogy between the church and the person of Christ is dominant, we find the stress placed on the perfection of the church, perhaps as the extension of the incarnation, and on the abidingness of the Spirit in the church.

In the course of this discussion, I hope to show that it is neither necessary nor possible to slight either of these aspects. The church is the community of believers, and the church is the Body of Christ. Though we may find it convenient to begin at one point or the other, a task of theology of the church is to find a way of dealing with the polar realities of its existence which shows how they in fact support and complement each other. In this spirit we may hope to focus at the same time on the doctrines of Christ, the Christian, and the church. We cannot suppose that at any point we have at hand complete formulas, on which to hang the rest of our thought. Rather we must try to think out together, and in constant relation to each other, our understandings of Christ, of his church, and of the Christian man—without confusion or identification, but in the conviction that thereby in all these realms our comprehension may be deepened and clarified. At the center of our particular interest, of course, remains the problem of the being of the church.

2. SOME CURRENT ANSWERS

It will be helpful to preface this problem further by taking brief and preliminary note of various "answers" to the question of the "paradox" of the church—all of which have some currency in our time and present interesting and significant parallels to certain interpretations of the incarnation. All of these, in my judgment, are inadequate, though the full reasons for this assessment can appear only in the course of the entire discussion. Five general perspectives which must be considered as tendencies of thought, or "types," may here be designated (i.e., they do not necessarily appear in pure form in any single concrete theological elaboration, but are useful in the understanding of particular presentations).

a. At one extreme is a view which has justly fallen into theological disfavor, but which only a generation ago was so commonly held as to come to expression even in such diverse figures as Edward Scribner Ames and John Gresham Machen.[1] Moreover, it still has a great currency in popular speech, both within and outside of church circles. According to this notion, the church is a voluntaristic association of individual believers, existing for the mutual assistance of members in their essentially private religious lives. It is an institution among other institutions, a member of the genus "religious society," whose existence is justified in terms of the service it renders to the individual Christian and/or to society in general. Although its purposes may be divine, although it may be modeled after and look to the creation on earth of an ideal fellowship whose principle and spirit are revealed in Christ, the actual church is a

[1] To be sure, Machen speaks of an invisible church, as the true company of the redeemed, the predestined of God. But this notion seems simply to stand alongside the concept of the visible (evangelical) church, which is defined as the voluntary association "of a number of persons who have come to agreement in a certain message about Christ and who desire to unite in the propagation of that message, as it is set forth in their creed on the basis of the Bible" (*Christianity and Liberalism*, p. 168).

For E. S. Ames, see, e.g., his essay in *Contemporary American Theology*, Second Series, ed. V. Ferm (New York, Round Table, 1933). This volume, together with the earlier companion volume, provides an illuminating indication of the extent to which American theology of the time was permeated by the general view of the church here under discussion.

The roots of this view are certainly to be traced back as far as the Enlightenment, but its modern form may be said to receive classic expression in Schleiermacher's *Speeches* (esp. Speech V). And following Schleiermacher, this conception became a dominant stream in 19th and 20th century thought.

humanly established and constituted community, **formed**
out of the assent of its members to certain common beliefs and purposes.

In such a conception of the church, it is patent that there
can be no real thought of "paradox" or polarity in the
church. Insofar as a tension remains, it is only in reference
to an ideal of what the church ought to become. And the
witness of the New Testament that the church not only
ought to be, but *is*, the True Israel and the New Humanity,
is compromised. This is an ecclesiological error roughly
parallel to the Ebionite error regarding the person of
Christ (and also to the anthropological error of Pelagian-
ism, which as Schleiermacher clearly saw, is a parallel to
Ebionitism [2]). Just as the confession of faith in Christ, the
Word made flesh, truly God and truly man, is lost when he
is understood exclusively in terms of his participation in
the common religious quest, so the dialectic of the church
is here abandoned in favor of a simple humanization of its
origin and continued existence. God does not call the
church into being. He calls individuals to faith in Christ,
and they organize a church.

b. The converse of this error appears, interestingly, in a
double form. It may take the form (1) of a divinization of
the historical faith, forms and structures of the church.
Thus the church, whatever may be the failings of its members, is itself beyond the ambiguities, contradiction and
imperfections which everywhere else characterize human

[2] Cf. *The Christian Faith*, par. 22.

existence. Its dogmatic pronouncements are infallible, its symbols and structure are irreformable. Human language, acts and patterns have been so elevated (or transformed) by the Holy Spirit that they share in the perfection and absoluteness of God himself. Sin and error cannot be attributed to the church as such, and this precisely in its manifest historical form.

(2) A similar judgment about the church takes the form of an apparently opposite assertion, *viz.*, that the church is really a purely "spiritual community." [3] Here a radical distinction is drawn between true church and institution, to the depreciation of the latter. Churchly institutions there are, but these are not the divinely established *ecclesia;* at best they are external means. Thus Brunner writes: "The New Testament *Ecclesia*, the fellowship of Jesus Christ, is a pure communion of persons and has nothing of the character of an institution about it. . . . The Ecclesia . . . is no institution. Therefore the church can never be the Ecclesia either by purification or recreation." [4] The implication of such views is that there is a "true" church, a perfect community, the *ecclesia* above and beyond (or per-

[3] Not necessarily to be identified with the notion of the "spiritual" (in contrast to institutional) unity of the church. This idea is so vague that it may also be associated with the previous church concept. Everything depends on the way "spiritual unity" is defined.

[4] E. Brunner, *The Misunderstanding of the Church* (London, Lutterworth, 1952), pp. 17, 107. This sort of statement seems to me to speak for a great deal of inchoate opinion, according to which the church is essentially free-floating and formless. That view is often expressed also in terms of the visible/invisible distinction, which is quite amenable to such interpretations.

haps within) the historical institutions, and it is to this that we ought to direct our concern. This alone is essential, for here is the true community called by God.

What unites these two seemingly quite divergent descriptions is the common judgment that the church (however one may seek to locate and identify it) does not essentially participate in the fallibility and corruption of our common human existence. Whether these elements are assigned simply to the members of the church (though how this can be done without affecting the whole of the church is a nice question!) or to accidental and secondary "institutions" is not for the moment important. In either case the church *qua* church is exempt. Both of these ways of thinking would seem to represent a kind of docetism of the church. The church has a human form which has ceased to be human,[5] or it has no properly human form at all. And this sort of docetism is basically only the obverse of the Ebionite error. Just as docetism and Ebionitism in Christology both rest upon a rejection of the paradox of the incarnation, so also these concepts of the church involve a denial of one or both of the fundamental dualities of the church. We may suspect that the pervasive tendency of a previous generation to reduce the church to a religious society has engendered a reaction leading toward

[5] An alternative statement would be that the church repeats or extends within itself the duality of the incarnation, and that the perfection of its humanity is the same as the perfection of the humanity of Christ. This notion, together with the basic principle of criticism mentioned here, will be discussed in subsequent chapters. It will be apparent that here, as at numerous other points in this chapter, I have dealt cursorily and summarily with matters to which fuller discussion must later be devoted.

the opposite view—which turns out to be only the other side of the same old error. And if Chalcedon forbids us to dissolve or ignore the depth of the problem of the person of Christ, it may also guard us against similar faults in thinking about the church.

c. A favorite Protestant way of seeking to avoid these errors, and be true to the polarities of the church's existence, is through the distinction "visible/invisible." The visible church is corrupt, the invisible church is holy; the visible church is the externally observable community (or communities), the invisible church is the one Body of Christ. At first glance, this seems an attractive suggestion, but the more closely one looks the more confusing it becomes. It can have, and has had, an enormous variety of meanings. It may refer to the company of true Christians as distinguished from the wider circle of nominal church members, either in the sense of a predestined few, or in the pietistic sense of the select group who have achieved perfection. This notion of a church within the church, however, is notoriously difficult to reconcile with the way in which the New Testament writers speak of the oneness and solidarity of the visible community and recognize the existence of sin within that community (see ch. IV). The distinction "visible/invisible" may also involve explicit or implicit appeal to a kind of "Platonic" essence, of which the visible churches are partial and defective images. But then the "true" church is a purely transcendent and heavenly reality, and this view turns out to be a way of giving up the tension very similar to that noted a moment ago (sect. *b*). Or, we are led toward a notion of two churches, the transcendent and the earthly, or the inner and the outer, more or less parallel with each other yet really different, and somehow or other to be brought into relation with each other. (Here the analogy to Christology may again be illuminating: to speak of two churches in this way seems to be quite as unacceptable as to speak of two Christs.) Once more, the distinction between the visible and the invisible church may be understood as referring to two ways of viewing the church, the church as viewed by faith and the church as seen apart from faith. But that becomes identical with another notion to be discussed in a moment.[6]

There is the further fundamental difficulty that the terminology of visible/invisible often has its real root in a problem different from the one now before us, *viz.*, the question of the bounds of the church, and particularly in connection with the doctrine that there is no salvation outside the church. But that is another question, to be dealt with in due course (see ch. VI). With respect to the present problem, we have to say that the terms "visible" and "invisible" offer little help. They do point to a real problem, but as soon as it is asked what they mean, they seem to blend, chameleon-like, into the coloration of one or another of the perspectives here outlined, or to lead to clearly unacceptable views, or simply to restate the prob-

[6] The term "invisible church" can also be used to refer to the company of saints in heaven, but that is an idea of a quite different order, and has no relation to our immediate problem.

lem, and that with such confusing connotations that I, for one, would gladly give them up.

d. In attempting to deal more precisely with the polarities of the church, and at the same time to avoid the unfortunate suggestions of a double church, or a Platonic essence, or a select group within the community, some would seek to define the problem simply in relation to ways of viewing the church. The key categories become the "hiddenness" of the church and the perception of faith. As the body of Christ and the work of the Holy Spirit, the church is hidden from the eyes of the world, but it is visible to the eyes of faith. It is one and the same church, the church in this world, which appears to the outward eye and to faith, but only faith can see that the disunited and imperfect body is nevertheless the one and holy people of God.

Such a view has obvious attractions. It begins at the right place, with the confession of faith in response to the act of God. It can help us to see vividly how the problems of Christ, of the church and of the believer come together: as there is a hiddenness, an *incognito*, in the life of Christ, so is the regenerate life of man and the life of the church hidden in God. As to the end of the earthly career of Christ, so to the end of our present lives and that of the church, the outward signs are never unambiguous. Only in faith is our vision corrected, so that we confess Jesus as the Lord, and recognize ourselves as redeemed men and the church as the true community of God.

But if we stop here, then we run the risk of accepting a doctrine of double truth; or we simply transfer the problem into the realm of epistemology, putting the duality in the eye of the beholder. Granted that we must view with the eyes of faith, we need also to ask, what does faith see? We have to inquire what it is which God has wrought in the incarnation, in the creation of a new humanity and a holy people. What are the "hidden" realities we confess, and how do they relate to the quite earthly and unholy realities so plainly evident to all?

e. The effort to go beyond such a purely noetic interpretation of the matter brings a further suggestion. This is the assertion simply of "both—and." As Christ is not only to be *viewed* as God and man, but *is* truly God and truly man, so the church *is* both the body of Christ and religious institution, both holy and sinful, and the believer *is* both sinner and a new being. But we can never say more here than "and." In particular, we cannot describe the "how" of the unities. The key to the pattern is given in the impenetrable mystery of the incarnation, which is embraced precisely by the word "and." That word designates the paradox, the inconceivability, the miracle, beyond which we cannot and must not try to go. The same is essentially true for the life of the children of God, in their togetherness in the church and in the life of each. The church is a quite humanly visible community of those who claim to have received God's revelation; it is *also* invisibly constituted by revelation, election, justification and sanctification, which make the church what it is. The believer is a man visible in himself, and yet just as that man he lives invisibly in Jesus Christ.[7] Thus, it may be argued, in our thought about the church we should profit by the wisdom of Chalcedon, confessing the mystery and affirming the paradox, but in no way trying to explain it.[8] This is not a counsel of despair, but a positive acknowledgment of the mystery of God's act, before which we bow in humility and adoration.

The objections to this perspective must be stated carefully, for it represents a clear-sighted effort to hold in true balance the dualities and tensions involved in faith's affirmations. Yet, without being presumptuous, we may hold such a view to be in itself inadequate. Not denying that the mysteries of faith are finally beyond our comprehension, we can and must explore them to the fullest possible extent. Otherwise, we risk falling into the trap of making paradox itself a theological principle, adopting this as the appropriate

[7] There are certain elements in Karl Barth's view of the church which seem to suggest this general perspective, but with the additional and decisive emphasis that the "apparent" church *becomes* the "real" or "actual" church always and only through the work of the Holy Spirit. The Holy Spirit raises up the human work to be the real church, which is visible, but only to faith visible as really the church. Thus Barth's view involves a more dynamic relation of the apparent and real church than the statement in the above paragraph might imply. It may also be added that although Barth uses the language of "apparent" (*scheinbar*) and "real" (*wirklich*), he in no way intends this in the sense of a Platonic essence and its image. Cf. esp. *KD*, IV/2, pp. 695ff.; also *Church Dogmatics* (Eng. tr.), I/2, pars. 13–15 and 18; and "The Real Church," *Scottish Journal of Theology*, III (1950), pp. 337f. See also below, ch. II, sect. 5.

[8] Such a statement is not wholly fair to Chalcedon. It is true that the intention of the Chalcedonian declaration was not to explain but to set boundaries and to exclude teachings which seemed to pervert the gospel. But this cannot be understood simply as a negative act, for in the attempt to insure adoration of the true mystery of Christ's being, that mystery was described in some quite definite and positive ways.

test of Christian affirmation. Or we reduce theology to a simple reiteration of biblical terms. Or we find ourselves using such utterly vague expressions as "in some real way" God was in Christ or Christ is present in the church, which really reveal only that we do not know exactly what we want to say.

The task of theology is precisely to try to avoid such ambiguities, to say so far as possible in *what* ways we refer to the church as sinful society and as people of God, to Christ as man and as God. The dimensions and terms of polarities and paradoxes need at least to be examined with all possible care. Moreover, no *a priori* limits can be set as to permissible concepts and categories of interpretation, for all language is human and all must be crucified with Christ in order to be vehicles of the Word. Thus one may have to range quite beyond the terms and figures of the Bible, in order precisely to interpret its meaning and to reply to questions which it urgently puts to those who subject themselves to the authority of the Word it proclaims.

If then, in these chapters, we try to go beyond the assertion merely that it is the eyes of faith alone which perceive Jesus to be the Christ and the church to be the body of Christ, or the confession that we simply confront "paradoxical" realities, it is not with the intention of rejecting what these judgments centrally affirm. The task is rather one of pursuing matters which these affirmations themselves present to us, and in particular such questions as the nature of the common humanity of Christ and his church, the relation of humanity and sin to the being of God in Christ and the new being of the community of faith (viewed from both ontological and eschatological perspectives), the meaning of participation in Christ, the relation of church and world, and the work of the Spirit in the church.

Chapter II

THE PEOPLE OF GOD

I. A RESPONDING PEOPLE

ACCORDING to a familiar interpretation of the Apostles' and Niceno-Constantinopolitan creeds, these symbols do not speak of believing "in" the church in the way in which faith in God the Father, Son and Holy Spirit is confessed. We believe "in" God the Father, "in" Jesus Christ, "in" the Holy Spirit, but not "in" the church in the same way. Thus the texts should be understood to read "I believe . . . the church," which suggests that the church surely belongs in the creed, as a part of our confession of faith, but in a different way from what has earlier been affirmed. We may believe "about" the church, or "within" the church, or we may believe it, but not, when we are talking of faith in its fullest dimensions, "in" it. Faith in the proper sense can have only God as its object, and we can really speak of faith in the church not "in itself" but only in relation to God in Jesus Christ.

Whether the language of these two creeds does itself require such a distinction is indeed open to question.[1] But

[1] E.g., J. N. D. Kelly, in *Early Christian Creeds* (1950), pp. 152ff., argues that the second century framers of "R" probably had no such distinction

42

it is significant that a long and weighty theological tradition, going back at least to Rufinus, has seen here an
expression of something absolutely fundamental in our conception of the church—namely, the creaturely being of the
church. Thus Paschasius Radbertus argued: "Therefore
do not let us say 'I believe *in* the Holy Catholic Church,'
but rather, cutting out the syllable 'in,' let us say 'I believe
the Holy Catholic Church' and 'the life everlasting' and
'the resurrection of the body.' Otherwise we shall seem to
'believe in' man, which is forbidden to us. We believe in
God alone and in His unique majesty." [2] Quite apart from
the question of the creedal syntax, this is a point to be insisted upon: the church stands unequivocally on our side of
the Creator/creature distinction.

To put it otherwise, we may speak of the *believing*
church. Whatever else the church may be, it is a community
of men responding to the gracious act of God. Whether
we emphasize that the church is a people *called of God* or

---

in mind. Rather, the series of affirmations were strung together with no
effort to draw precise distinctions of this sort between them. (At the
same time, that does not make the distinction illegitimate.)

[2] Cited in Henri de Lubac, *The Splendour of the Church*, p. 16. De Lubac
has assembled an impressive array of testimony on this point (cf. *ibid.*
pp. 13ff.), and himself emphasizes it strongly. Cf. also pp. 69ff., where
de Lubac properly insists on the duality of the *calling* of the people
and the *people* called. Though we may not be able to go all the way
with de Lubac in his development of these fundamental judgments, it
is nonetheless a cause for rejoicing that in this initial affirmation, Roman
Catholic, Protestant, and Orthodox can unite. (On the Orthodox side,
Professor G. Florovsky, at the meeting of the Theological Commission
on Christ and the Church, in Evanston, 1954, strongly warned against
denying the reality of the human response of faith—a warning directed
against certain lines of Protestant thought!)

that it is a people *answering*, and we must do both, we are
equally concerned with a concrete, earthly people—and
if we do not make this explicit and hold to it, we fall at once
into a docetic, or at least Arian, translation of the church
out of the realm of human existence. The Augsburg Confession has the merit of making this quite clear, when it
defines the church as "the assembly of all believers, in which
the gospel is purely preached and the sacraments rightly
administered according to the gospel" (Art. VII, following
the German text, but the Latin is equally clear on this
point). That is, the church is defined as the visible community of believers, in which certain things take place. And
these happenings in the community are understood, not as
some secret possession of truth or hidden happening in the
sacrament, but first of all as the quite concrete vocal act of
preaching and the equally concrete presenting of the sacraments.[3]

One would think it unnecessary to emphasize such an
obvious fact about the church as its real humanity. Yet in
our new concern with a theology of the church, and especially in reaction to notions of the church as merely a con-
tractual association of like-minded individuals, we may be
tempted to deny just this truth. One even hears it asserted
that "the church is divine, not human!" But a similar pre-
supposition is involved when the "social factors" in the
church's life are placed simply under the rubric of "sinful

[3] Cf. Edmund Schlink, *Theologie der lutherischen Bekenntnisschriften*,
2te Aufl., Muenchen, 1947, pp. 269ff. The emphasis upon the people believing is characteristic of Luther. Cf. e.g., T. F. Torrance, *Kingdom and
Church*, Edinburgh, 1956, p. 57.

divisions." Or, in eagerness to affirm that the church is sustained wholly by Christ, one may tend to deny all significance to human response. Now it may be perfectly true that *we* do not preserve the church, for the church existed long before any of us and will continue long after we are dead. But we must understand what is meant by this assertion. It is one thing to say that the church can exist without any one of us; it is quite another thing to say that the church can exist without *anyone*. That is false. The church cannot exist without anyone, without the human response of faith. Thus the idea of an "eternal" church can be maintained, if at all, only in a carefully qualified sense. And if we wish to say that the church existed in Jesus Christ alone, and particularly in Christ on the cross, when the community of disciples was scattered and despairing,[4] then we must recognize that it existed there precisely in the believing humanity of our Lord. Moreover, this was not an existence of the church simply in the faith of an individual. Even there the church existed as a community. The church can be found in Christ because he embodies the people in himself, as its representative, head and substitute, because he is the first-born of brethren and the spring of life for the community, because he incorporates us into his humanity, so that we have community with him and in him.

But this leads us to the problem which must be discussed

[4] Cf. the familiar figure of the hour-glass, an idea expressed, e.g., by O. Cullmann in *Christ and Time*, pp. 115ff., where the community is viewed as progressively narrowing from the people of Israel to embodiment in the person of Christ, and thence broadening out in the post-resurrection community.

in detail later (ch. V). At the moment I am concerned only to stress the character of the church as a *people* believing. The significance of this is shown in an unexpected way in the New Testament. I refer to those passages in which the word *ecclesia* is used in an apparently casual and "neutral" sense: the seven churches in Asia (Rev), the "church throughout all Judea and Galilee" (Acts 9:31), "every church" (Acts 14:23), "all the churches" of the Gentiles (Rom 16:4) or "of Jesus Christ" (Rom 16:16), "the whole church" (Rom 16:23), the persecuted church (Acts 8:1, 3), the manifold references to the church simply as the company of Christians, and to particular churches in cities and areas (notably at the beginning and ending of Paul's letters). So also the references to "the church in their house" (e.g., Rom 16:5; I Cor 16:19; Col 4:15; Phil 1:2); to the "assembly" (Acts 15:30); and even to the church in the sense of the group assembled for worship (e.g., I Cor 11:18 and 14:4, 19, 23, 28, 35). In such designations as these, the primary reference is apparently simply to the concrete company of Christian persons, and the church is not described in any particular way. Thus most of these references are often held to be of no special ecclesiological significance. On the contrary, however, these passages are important precisely because they express what is taken for granted throughout the New Testament, that the Church is patently and indisputably (we might even say, first of all) a human community responding. This belongs to the essence, the ontology, of the church. That is to be seen also in the central New Testament meaning of the word "ec-

clesia," signifying the people called forth by God.[5] In the
relationship denoted by this concept, one pole is constituted
by "the people." In this respect, among others, the being
of the church is precisely like that of the covenant people
of Israel.

The same point can be illustrated by many of the ways
in which the New Testament describes the people of God:
as sons, heirs, brothers, disciples, followers, witnesses, confessors, believers, faithful ones, ambassadors, pilgrims, free
men, slaves, servants, stewards, ministers, friends, sons of
Abraham; as a holy nation, chosen race, commonwealth,
colony of heaven, family of God, God's beloved, Israel,
etc. Various descriptions of the relation of Christ and the
church are equally suggestive: master and disciples, shepherd and flock, bridegroom and bride, physician and the
sick, judge and the judged, chastizer and chastized, etc.
In all these ways of speaking, as well as in others here less
explicit (e.g., the body, the new creation, the temple, the
New Jerusalem, the field, the building, the way, the royal
priesthood), the New Testament never loses touch with the
fact that what is designated in such exalted language is a
concrete community of people. Thus the assertions inter-
mingle with exhortations. Whether we consider these terms
as "images" or as more than images, their reference is to
the responding people. It is they who are so described.
When St. Paul writes of the body of Christ, he is writing

---

[5] Cf. esp. K. L. Schmidt, article on *Ekklesia*, in Kittel's *Theologisches
Wörterbuch zum neuen Testament*, III, pp. 502ff., and G. Johnston, *The
Doctrine of the Church in the New Testament*.

to and about a group taken for granted to be a body of people.[6]

The matter can also be expressed in reference to the rule of God. The church is not itself the objective rule of God. Though one might affirm that the kingdom of God is apprehended only in the church, that to apprehend the Kingdom is to be in the church, or even that God's realm is coextensive with the church (which I should certainly not assert; see ch. VI), he must still say that the church stands over against God's rule as a "subjective pole," as the community which acknowledges and lives in response to God's rule. The church may be fully dependent on God's act, but it is not simply God acting. It is a people believing, worshipping, obeying, witnessing. Thus we can and must make fast at the outset our understanding of the church as a body or community of human beings, albeit existing in response to the activity of God. In this sense, the ontology of the church means in the first instance the humanly subjective pole of the relationship.[7]

[6] One might be tempted to say that in such expressions, the people are substantive, and "body of Christ" or "called of God" adjectival. But this, as is implied in the argument below, would be a misleading and finally false distinction because it fails to take account of what it means to be a people, i.e., a community.

[7] This ought to warn us against a simple parallelism of the nature of the church with the nature of Christ, especially if one holds, as often asserted, that the eternal Word is the "subject" of the humanity of Christ. *Precisely this cannot be said of the church.* The "subject" of our believing is neither the Logos nor the Holy Spirit, but our own finite selfhood. This is not, I think, contradicted by the doctrine of our participation in Christ, or his substitutionary incorporation of us in his humanity (cf. ch. V). At the same time, we are required to re-examine the concepts of *anhypostasia* and *enhypostasia* in relation to the person of Christ (cf. ch. III, sect. 4).

2. THE PEOPLE AND SOCIAL PROCESS

Taking this judgment as a beachhead for our understanding of the church, we must strike out in several related directions. First, mention may be briefly made of the profoundly social, communal, or corporate nature of the believer's relation to Jesus Christ, which is implicit in what has been said so far. In the New Testament there is no "private" relation to Christ; to be in Christ is to be in the church. For example, it is often very difficult, if not impossible, to say whether a particular term is being used to describe the Christian or the church. Indeed, the effort to carry through such a distinction is an imposition of alien categories on the New Testament. There we find no great concern to say what belongs to the individual believer and what to the church. The individual is, *qua* believer, in the church. To be sure, the gospel confronts him with the necessity for decision, and the act of faith is an act which he himself is constrained to make, but the gospel comes to him in the witness of the church, and the acknowledgment of faith takes place in the context of the faith of the whole body of believers. Similarly, the concept of discipleship in the gospels refers not to a merely individualistic relation of a follower to a leader but to participation in a community. Christian existence is designated as membership in a family, a household, a colony, a flock, a race, and a body. It is membership in Israel, and the New Testament view of life of the Christian can only be understood in the light of the Old Testament conception of the solidarity of Israel.

The question of the relation of individual and community is one which must be explored at length, and its full depth is reached only as one grapples with the meaning of participation in Christ and with the notion of the body of Christ (see ch. V). At the moment, however, the argument leads in the direction of a somewhat different facet of the church's being. This is suggested by the frequency and ease with which, in the New Testament, the community of human beings called the church is described in terms drawn from other common social entities, e.g., city, nation, kingdom, commonwealth, race, household, people, colony, tribes, and family. (Of course, a variety of non-personal images are also used in referring to the wholeness of the church, such as flock, temple, tree, field, building, as well as body. But it would appear that the most widely used terms, when specific reference is made to the community as such, are drawn from other social groups.) Significant here is the New Testament writers' lack of hesitation in using such designations. The church is, to be sure, unique among all communities: it is "the people" in contrast to "no people," the people of God in contrast to other tribes and tongues and nations and peoples, the household of God in contrast to other families, etc. But the uniqueness of the church does *not* lie in its having ceased to be a community meaningfully described in the same terms applied to other and familiar human groups.

To take a step further, as we look at the life of the church depicted in the New Testament, we see processes of social interaction which are characteristic of social groups in general. A traveling representative visits cities in Asia Minor, gathers together groups of adherents, and appoints leaders in each group to supervise and guide its further development (e.g., Acts 14:21–23). Disagreements and problems of discipline arise in the communities, which are dealt with by letter or messenger or personal visitation. Decisions of moment are made, in choosing delegates for certain missions, in determining fundamental conditions of membership (cf. Acts 15; Gal 2), in allocating spheres of work and responsibility (i.e., jurisdictional problems) (Gal 2:9), in selecting associates for special tasks (e.g., Acts 6:1ff.), and in filling a vacancy in the original core of leadership (the lots were not cast until after preliminary selection on the basis of certain clearly defined qualifications, cf. Acts 1:15–26). Such decisions are taken in consultation among the leaders (e.g., Acts 15:6ff.; Gal 2:1ff.), or (apparently) by the people on recommendation of the leaders (cf. Acts 6:2, 5; II Cor 8:19 ?), even by majority vote (II Cor 2:6). Apparently loose and casual organization gradually gives way to more formal, explicit and uniform ordering.[1]

All this activity goes on, to be sure, in a certain context expressing fundamental convictions, memories and expectations of the community, but it also represents the sort of processes common to all human societies.[2] And this is

[1] Cf., e.g., John Knox, The Early Church and the Coming Great Church, esp. chs. 1, 4 and 5.

[2] That certain developments, e.g., Paul's call to Macedonia (Acts 16:9f.), are represented as following from the immediate instruction of the Holy Spirit, without reference and indeed quite obviously contrary to "ordinary" human patterns, is no disproof of the point being made here. We

throughout characteristic of the life of the church, whether we think of conciliar decisions on matters central to faith, or of the formation of the canon, or of the development of liturgy, or of formulation of rules of discipline, or of the selection and ordering of the ministry. In this respect, the decisions of a church board of deacons or a Roman consistory concerning the life of the church are not different from the decision of the apostles and elders, with the whole church, to send men to Antioch along with Paul and Barnabas (Acts 15:22—they did it because "it seemed good" to them). And these in turn reflect social patterns expressed also in corporation boards of directors, political parties and legislatures, secret societies, 4-H clubs, primitive tribes and service organizations.

Precisely at this point, more formal sociological analysis of the church becomes pertinent, for this is only the same observation on a larger and more systematic scale. We may note, in relation, e.g., to Malinowski's categories, how the church resembles other social groups in its amenability to functional analysis, how it also achieves cultural relevance necessarily through organized activities, how in it also a "charter," rules and norms, personnel, and material apparatus relate to its activities and functions.[3] Or, we may

---

may suspect a persistent tendency, especially on the part of Luke (and associated with his general preference for the more unusual manifestations of the Spirit), to move immediately to a statement of the ultimate source of direction for the church, ignoring the more mundane "human" agency. Be that as it may, there is ample evidence in the NT for the operation of precisely these ordinary social processes, and that at most crucial points.

[3] Cf. B. Malinowski, *A Scientific Theory of Culture.*

view, with Weber, the presence in the church of "communal" and "associative" principles of social relationship, or the way in which patterns of order are legitimatized: through tradition, through "affectual" assent to the validity of what is newly presented (or revealed), through "rational" belief in absolute values expressed, e.g., in natural law, or through "legal" establishment.[4] Or we may note how general patterns of transmission of authority are reflected in the church, and in particular how both at the beginning and in subsequent movements of renewal a pattern of development appears (as in other social groups) from personal and charismatic leadership to more "rationalized" and "bureaucratic" concepts of office (or perhaps charisma is institutionalized and transmitted by the laying on of hands).

Moreover, we can see the way in which at any given time and place the church reflects the patterns and natures of other social groupings in the culture in which it exists, and tends to reflect in itself changes in those patterns. It takes into itself patterns of national, family, social, economic, and educational life. This may be most clear to us in terms of the contemporary American church, because it has been extensively studied there; but when and where has it not been true of the church, whether in the Far East, in Latin America, in medieval Europe, in the Byzantine east or the Roman west, or even in the first century church? Attempts to segregate the church from the general social life have

---

[4] Cf. Max Weber, *The Theory of Social and Economic Organization*, esp. Part III.

usually meant the absolutization of some previous social form, and where new patterns of community have emerged, they have not been without resemblance to "non-church" forms, particularly in respect of their continuing development.

The involvement of the church in social process may be illustrated in a specific way by the changing conceptions of the primary (though not exclusive) role of the ministry. The task of the minister has been understood basically as that of pastoral rule, exercised through church discipline and especially through the penitential office (as in the *Pastoral Rule* of Gregory the Great); it has been conceived as a priestly or sacramental office, concerned chiefly with the dispensation of sacramental grace and the saving of souls from hell (as in the Roman church); it has been viewed as essentially the work of preaching the word of forgiveness and reconciliation with God (as in the Reformation), or more narrowly as the task of evangelistic conversion (as in the Wesleyan and pietistic movements and in nineteenth century revivalism).[5] What is significant in this de-

[5] Cf. H. R. Niebuhr, *The Purpose of the Church and Its Ministry*, pp. 58ff. Speaking of the present scene in America, Niebuhr writes: "As the polity of all the churches, whether they are episcopal, presbyterian or congregational by tradition, has been modified in the direction of the political structures of Canada and the United States, so the institutional status and authority of the ministry are being modified in the direction of the democratic type of political, educational and economic executive or managerial authority." Niebuhr also makes precisely the appropriate judgment upon this development (and its parallels in the church's history): "The question is not whether the ministry will reflect the institutional forms of leadership in the world but whether it will reflect these with the difference that Christian faith and church life require; . . ." *op. cit.*, p. 90. Cf. also H. R. Niebuhr and D. D. Williams, eds., *The Ministry in Historical Perspectives*.

velopment for our present consideration is the way in which it shows the intimate interrelation of the church with its cultural environment, for these patterns did not suddenly appear full-blown, nor were they "externally" imposed nor simply deduced from scripture, but sprang out of the situation, the needs, experiences, traditions and practices of the age.

3. A PEOPLE IN TIME

The church is not only a community exhibiting in its life familiar patterns of social interaction, it is also and essentially an *historical* community. This is most specifically expressed in the New Testament in terms of the involvement of the church in the life and history of Israel, which appears both in explicit affirmations of continuity with Israel and in the use of such figures as "people," "nation," "twelve tribes," "holy city," "kingdom," and numerous others carried over from Old Testament usage. In this respect, as well as in its continuing existence, the church participates in history in a manner quite like other human communities.

What I have in mind here is not the uniqueness of the events in which the church finds its origin and meaning, their historical character as unrepeatable happenings—though that is an important assertion—but rather the inextricable relation of a community to the time process. There is no mature community without a past, indeed without a memory of several generations, or without the expectation of a future. It is not too much to say that history is our primary mode of identification in community. Or, as Royce has put it, "true community is essentially a product of a time process. A community has a past and will have a future. Its more or less conscious history, real or ideal [I should say real *and* ideal], is a part of its very essence." [1] As the human self is a being with a past, so human community comes into being only through common experience in time; as selves can share a common past, they become one in their history. (In this sense time does not separate, but unites.) With a certain justification, one might speak of the birthday of the church on Pentecost, but it would not and could not have been the same church apart from the total "process" of the coming of God in Christ, nor apart from the preceding life of Israel. [2]

The temporal character of the Christian community is expressed in several ways. As already implied, it is seen in the shared memory of certain crucial events. Just as the national existence of a Rome or an England is characterized by the recollection of events viewed as determinative for the life of the state, so the church is informed by the memory of Jesus of Nazareth, of preaching of the kingdom

[1] J. Royce, *The Problem of Christianity*, II, p. 37. This view has been more recently developed by H. R. Niebuhr, especially in *The Meaning of Revelation*, ch. II. But its roots go back to Augustine.

[2] Thus it is a mistake to argue about the precise date of the "origin" of the church, whether this is to be identified with the calling of the disciples, or Peter's confession, or the community of resurrection witness, or the Ascension, or Pentecost. The possibility of arguing for any one of these derives from the fact that each is essential to the existence of the church. The error arises from the tendency to conceive these as a series of more or less discrete events and acts of God. It would be better to speak of this as a single act or event, embracing a span of time, through which the church is called into being.

of God, of demand for repentance and faith, of teaching and healing and forgiving sins, of crucifixion and resurrection, and of pentecostal empowering of the disciples. The church recalls, as an indispensable part of its life, the history of Israel—of patriarchs, of bondage in Egypt and liberation, of Moses, of prophets, of law given of God, and of the promise of a Messiah. The church *is* "the Israel of God" (Gal 6:16), "Abraham's offspring, heirs according to the promise" (Gal 3:29), "the true circumcision" (Phil 3:3). It recounts the deeds of God in Israel, and the faith and disobedience of the people, as essential to its own story.[3] Similarly, the church of subsequent generations builds also on the memory of its life since Pentecost.

The common memories of this social group, as of others, are closely linked with shared patterns of belief and expectation, of interpretation and meaning, through which past and present experience is understood. Community does not persist simply through temporal contiguity, but through the communication of common values, judgments, norms and hopes. The continuity of the church with Israel, writes Paul, consists not in the descent of the flesh but in the maintenance of the promise (cf. Rom 9:6ff.; Gal 3:29). And the author of Hebrews declares that we are of God's house "if we hold fast our confidence and pride in our hope" (Heb 3:6).

But continuity of meaning (or faith) is no simple matter, as St. Paul could well testify. And in every community, the

---

[3] In this connection, one thinks especially of Heb 11, of Stephen's sermon in Acts 7, and of course of Rom 9–11.

fundamental patterns of interpretation for its past and present life, the central beliefs and aspirations, are sooner or later given some explicit formulation, whether in scripture, creed, constitution, by-laws, or stable oral tradition. Some such normative statement seems to play an indispensable role in the existence in time of any genuine human community.[4] These more or less explicit formulations of meaning become means of communication or transmission in time in the community. This does not occur simply by virtue of their formulation, but through a continual process of interchange—as the authority of past statements is reaffirmed actively in the community, and as the community is given continuity of meaning from one generation to another through the medium of such fixed points of reference.

This process involves not only verbal symbols but also significant rites and ceremonies. In the church that means especially the sacraments (thus the Reformers insisted that scripture, preaching and sacraments alike proclaim the gospel). Word of scripture and sacramental act fill similar roles as vehicles of communication. We may speak of them thus as signs or symbols, not now thinking of their reference to "eternal realities," but simply of an undeniable function they perform in the life of the community. They are outward signs through which convictions, hopes, memories and loyalties are conveyed from person to person and from generation to generation.[5] They are at the same time signs

[4] In the following description of the functional significance of scripture and sacrament as communal symbols, I am much indebted to my colleague, Prof. James Gustafson.
[5] No matter how much one might want to emphasize sacraments as veri-

to be interpreted, in relation to each other and in relation to the total experience of the community. They are thus continually "given" meaning by the community and their meaning fluctuates, within limits determined by the character of the sign. Yet the fact that they have in themselves a certain fixity or stability is the key to their role in the communal life; [6] it is furthermore the mark of their indispensability. Without some kind of authoritative statements, or symbolic rites, or both, through which the basic convictions of the group are continually re-presented, it does not seem possible for a community to maintain itself in time. As words and gestures are necessary for communication between individuals, so communal signs are needed for the continuing life of a social group.[7] It may even be said that "society lives by its symbols." And "these are not idle or interchangeable. The Cross is not interchangeable with the Crescent or the Lotus. The Cross is one thing, and the Swastika is another. The Sheaf of Wheat is one thing, and the Fascis is another. The 'Battle Hymn of the Republic' is one thing, and the 'Internationale' is another. The

---

table channels of grace, apart from the apprehension of the recipient, it would be absurd to divorce their efficacy entirely from the consciousness of the church—and I do not suppose that any one has ever proposed to do this.

[6] Cp. K. Barth's comments on the importance of the *written* form of scripture, e.g., *Church Dogmatics,* I/1, pp. 117f.; I/2, pp. 581f.

[7] That this applies to the church is amply shown in the history of the Quakers and the would-be purely "spiritual" movements in the church. None of these have in fact been able to dispense altogether with such fundamental signs, but to the extent to which they have approximated such an end, they have either rapidly vanished or so fundamentally altered as to be no longer recognizably the same community.

Lincoln Memorial is one thing, and the Tomb of Lenin is another." [8]

Finally, in understanding the existence of communities in time, we must note that continuity in social life is bound up with institutional structures, especially relating to the regularization and succession of leadership. Any attempt to divorce "community" from "institution," except for purposes of analysis, is futile. There is no historical community which does not order its common life in some kind of explicit pattern, through which it seeks to express its ultimate faith and norms and to provide for their maintenance and transmission. With reference to the Christian community, this means, of course, church "order" and ministry.

4. THE POINT OF VIEW

Thus far in this chapter I have been trying to show how the church must be viewed, not only at first glance or on the surface, but fundamentally, as a body of human beings, an observable social group, whose life is characterized by social processes common to other societies and which exists necessarily in time in a manner conformable to all significant human communities. Now the question at once arises, what is the relation of this to the witness of faith? From what perspective are such observations made? In looking at the church in this way, are we abandoning the dictum of Paul: "From now on, therefore, we regard no one from a human

[8] Amos N. Wilder, "The Church's New Concern with the Arts," *Christianity and Crisis*, XVII, 2 (Feb. 18, 1957), p. 14.

point of view" (II Cor 5:16)? Do we adopt a purely "human" point of view, the vantage point of the observer, the "neutral," "external," uncommitted standpoint of the sociologist, the social philosopher or the historian? Are we concerned only with "external history" in contrast to the "internal history" seen by faith?

It is my conviction that such questions must be answered firmly in the negative. This way of viewing the church is not extraneous to the perspective of faith. It is not merely a so-called "objective" view of the church, irrelevant to the theological task of understanding the "true nature" of the people of God. On the contrary, precisely *in faith* have we to see the church in this way. That the church is subject to sociological analysis is not a fact to be deplored, as representing an accidental and rather unfortunate aspect of the church's being. It is of positive import for theology, for this is but a reflection of the nature of the church as a humanly concrete body of responding people [1]—which nature, as I have tried to show, is clearly recognized in the New Testament. *For faith, this human-ness of the believing community belongs to the ontology of the church,* to its very being as the church. When we view the church in sociological or philosophico-historical categories we do not suddenly cease to be believers and think as uncommitted observers; rather we remain unitary human beings seeking

[1] Thus investigation such as that of the Study Commission on Institutionalism does not represent simply "sociological" and "practical" concerns, somehow ancillary to the "theological" problems of the nature and unity of the church. This is itself theological study, the results of which are very much relevant to our theology of the church.

to deepen our understanding of this peculiar community. We maintain precisely the position of those whose life is determined in response to God, and who *in that response* try to describe their existence.

If it be allowed that faith judges the church to be truly a community of and among men, which humanity is expressed in significant patterns of human togetherness in space and time, i.e., through real participation in social process and in historical life, then certain consequences follow immediately. For one thing, we can have nothing to do with an "occasionalist" view of the church. According to such a notion, one would think of the church not simply as dependent on the will of God for its existence at every moment, but also as finding its continuity in time and its unity in space purely in the direct action of God. All significant relations in the church exist only as God immediately wills them. That is, the church is continually created anew from one moment to the next and in every place.[2] Such a view does not really celebrate the majesty of God and his Lordship over the church, but only defines lordship in a very narrow and unbiblical way. In contrast to that sort of talk, the church, as composed of human beings in real social and historical relation to one another, must be affirmed to have a reality in itself, located squarely in the stream of socio-historical existence. This is not to declare the independence of the church from God, nor to deny

---

[2] This notion has obvious affinities with an occasionalist view of creation, but there are those who with no thought of the latter would nevertheless describe the church in the way suggested.

his freedom to act anew in and upon the church; it is to say that the church has its dependence on God as genuine social and historical movement.

Again, it must be affirmed that the relation of the Christian to Christ cannot be defined without reference to the historical career of the church. Contemporaneity with Christ is not simply a "vertical" or "mystical" confrontation. If it is that, it is necessarily at the same time a relation in and through a very complex fabric of personal and social existence in time—through, we may say, immanent historical reality.[3] But more of this later, when we come to speak of participation in Christ and the work of the Spirit.

The recognition that the being of the church is really a finite, historical being also forbids us to be satisfied with notions of the unity of the church as purely "invisible" or "transcendent" or "spiritual." However fervently we confess that the unity of the church is given it by God, we must still ask after the fleshly, i.e., social embodiment. And if the unity has its essential reality in Jesus Christ himself, we must yet interpret this in some clear relation to historical process.[4]

[3] It is certainly the merit of Roman Catholic theology, and of Schleiermacher!, to hold firmly to this point; though we may have to say that neither does it in the right way.

[4] That is the justification for such judgments about church unity as the following, made by representative organs of the World Council of Churches, as cited by W. A. Visser 't Hooft in *The Ecumenical Review*, VIII, 1 (Oct. 1955), p. 5: "This unity must be manifest to the world"; "full church unity must be based on a large measure of agreement in doctrine"; "sacramental communion is a necessary part of full church unity," as is also "a ministry acknowledged by every part of the church." (The selection of these statements and partial statements from Visser 't

5. THE PEOPLE UNDER GOD

Such judgments, and indeed the whole course of our argument in this chapter, raise at once the question how this "immanent" historical reality of the church is at the same time a reality "under God," a people dependent on God, an act not of men but of God. In part, this question must be dealt with in the next chapter, for the essential humanity of the church must be seen in the light of, and itself helps us to understand, the manner of God's act and presence in Jesus Christ. The historical particularity of the church is analogous to the historical figure of Christ; the being of the Son in Christ and the work of the Holy Spirit in the church are inseparable. As God humbles himself to assume real humanity in the incarnation, so in the church he does not scorn to meet us *in* the history in which we live.

Yet the root question is also posed directly in the terms with which we began. To speak of a responding community is to affirm that there is an object to which response is made. *Ecclesia* means both *convocatio* and *congregatio*, the calling together and the community constituted by that calling. This polarity must be vigorously maintained, and if, in accordance with the New Testament, we make fast our

---

Hooft's list does not imply any adverse judgment on the other statements cited.)

It is sometimes affirmed that the greater unity we have, the less it needs to be specified. While one may recognize an element of truth in this sort of statement, it cannot be taken strictly without denying central elements of our understanding of community—and the inferences which can be drawn from this statement may be very dangerous.

understanding of the church as truly human community, we must also see it properly as the people *of God*. For it is at least equally clear in the New Testament that this human community is wholly dependent on God. It is his creation, his act. We are brethren just because we "share in a heavenly call" (Heb 3:1). Those who were once no people have been made a people, a race, a priesthood, a nation, by being called out of darkness and by receiving mercy (I Peter 2:9f.). Their community is constituted by their being called, and justified, and glorified (Rom 8:31).

All that we can say, then, about the genuine sociality and historicity of the common life of the church must refer also and primarily to the working of God. It is by the grace of Christ that the church is upheld. Apart from the faithfulness of God in Christ and the indwelling of the Holy spirit, the church could not be or continue to be the church. Thus the church does not claim anything for herself, but only for Christ. She acknowledges herself to exist only in God's election, in his covenant mercy, to be what she is from and by the Word. The church's being *congregatio* is meaningless apart from God's *convocatio*. Yet, *congregatio* must not be swallowed up in *convocatio*, nor the visible spatio-temporal form and extension minimized by exclusive preoccupation with the working of the Holy Spirit. The humanly social existence of the church is not simply to be contrasted with a "true" existence of the church in Christ, nor the association in love and brotherliness opposed to common life in Christ. These poles of the church's being are not to be set in opposition to each other, but

thought into each other. The humanly social principle of
unity in the church is not in conflict with the unity given
it by Christ, but is a corollary and expression of the latter.
The being of the church in Christ, its calling and sustenance
by God, is precisely the ground of its being this particular
humanly social and historical common life.[1]

[1] It is in this area that we must raise the fundamental question regarding
Karl Barth's doctrine of the church elaborated under the rubric of the
"real" church (*die wirkliche Kirche*, in contrast to the "apparent"
church, *die scheinbare Kirche*). (Cf. *KD*, IV/2, 695ff.) It is true that
Barth speaks of maintaining the duality of the church as both work of
God and work of man (e.g., pp. 697f.). But considered simply as work
of man, the church is only apparent church. Only through the work of
the Holy Spirit does the church come to be real church; the Holy Spirit
erects the church and her work to be real church (698ff.), so that the
church corresponds to her name, corroborates her essence and is worthy
of the biblical titles (cf. 725). Thus throughout the paragraph on the
Holy Spirit and the building up of the Christian community (pp. 695–
824), Barth continually insists that it is only God who builds up, who
makes the church to be true and appropriate presentation of the salvation
of mankind, true servant of his goal, and thereby really church.

The objection to be raised here is not against the assertion of the dependence of the church on God, but against the way in which existence
in that dependence is described. It is affirmed that the real church exists
in the event of her erection to be church (e.g., p. 725). This is not intended
in an occasionalist sense, but nevertheless involves the danger of dissolving
(i.e., in terms of theological significance) the *congregatio* into pure
convocatio. True, for Barth, it is the concrete historical community which
becomes the real church, but the emphasis is so strongly placed on the
identity of the real church with what the Holy Spirit makes out of the
empirical community that the latter is no longer real church, but only
possibility of church.

The dimensions of the problem may perhaps best be seen when we
recognize that in asking about the being (the ontology) of the church,
we are asking about ourselves as Christians, as members of the community. And in faith, in response to God, we have to say that our being
such is wholly dependent on him. Thus Barth rightly insists upon the act
of God in erecting the church, and fears lest the church should claim
something for herself. Yet precisely in this situation it is we who confess
our dependence on God, and must in theology describe this reality also.

How is this to be understood? Here, I think, we are helped by our previous analysis of the church as community.

1) First of all, we see the church in indissoluble relation to the very temporal, socio-historical act of God in the person of Jesus Christ. The church is indisputably formed around that concrete historical figure. The event to which it looks back as decisive for its existence is the event of the life, death and resurrection of this particular man. The risen Christ who is present with and in the church is none other than the Jesus of Nazareth who was present in the flesh (it is not just "any" resurrection that the church

---

Therefore at least two further things must be said: (1) God makes us truly beings in our dependence on him. We (and that means the church) are not God's act as such, but finite reality which God has called into being and permits to exist over against himself. Thus the genuine creaturely being of the church must be insisted on. (2) The church is, *qua* church, characterized by both grace and sin. Barth really gives up the "paradox" by defining the church determined by sin as only apparent church, and only the church determined by grace as real church. But it is possible to maintain this distinction only by neglecting to give proper account of the reality (one may say, substantiality) of the believer and the community as subject of faith.

This defect of Barth's view may also be related to his continued penchant for interpretation in terms of the subject-predicate relation (cf., e.g., IV/2, 769ff., 777f., 747f.). When the matter is so put, then of course this order is essential. Thus the church is the predicate of Christ, and not vice versa. But certainly this pattern of relations cannot be permitted to stand alone or without correction as a representation of the relation of Christ and the church (or of God and man in Jesus Christ). This pattern is useful in emphasizing the primacy of *God's* act, but in itself it has no place for the essential mutuality and reciprocity of divine and human in the person of Jesus Christ (which Barth emphasizes strongly, and it is part of the greatness of his Christology) and in the church. At this point, it seems that Barth's fondness for the grammatical analogy becomes an obstruction to his own interpretation.

celebrates, but the resurrection of *this* man, cf. Lk 24:19ff.).
It is he who is remembered, the one who was crucified
under Pontius Pilate. So the church has its *being* as the
community which remembers him. As its formative memory
is given in time, so also the faith and expectation of the
church are given to it in the historical event of Christ's
words and deeds, his living, dying and rising again. Also,
of course, the church is the church only as it remembers
the life of Israel and knows itself to be continuous with
that history; the people of the Messiah are those who both
remember and expect the Messiah. But this only strengthens
the point that we dare not ignore the historical means
which God has chosen. Both in Israel as the chosen preparation, and in Jesus of Nazareth as the fulfillment of God's
redemptive act, the dependence of the church upon God
is in the first instance and essentially a dependence upon his
act in history. In this respect, the church has its being in
Christ just because it is a community in time.

2) The supposed contrast between the church as an historical phenomenon and as a people called of God (or
existing in Christ and filled by the Spirit) is further overcome as we recognize that the "phenomenological" existence of the church is itself decisively determined by the
community's understanding of itself in relation to God in
Jesus Christ.[2] That is to say, the participation of the church
in the pattern of human community in general does not

---

[2] R. Bultmann, *Theology of the New Testament*, vol. II., pp. 96f., points
out that this is especially true of the unity of the primitive church, which
sharply distinguished it from the mystery cults.

mean that the character and development of the church is simply a function of external historical factors and laws; rather, what comes to expression in real historicity is none the less the peculiar relation of this people to God in Jesus Christ.

This relation of dependence, of having its being in God, is thus on the one side the active expression in the community of its faith and love to God. That the faith and love of the church is directed always to God means that even as an historical community it looks not only backward and forward and around but upward. To use Augustine's language about the city of God, the love of this city is for the eternal. If a *civitas* is defined as a community having a common object of love,[3] and this but points in another way to the nature of historical community as we have described it, then the *civitas* which is the church is defined by the God whom it loves. Its memories and hopes always have a more than immanently historical reference; the Jesus whom it remembers is acknowledged as the Son of God, he is at the same time the living Lord present in the church, and he is the one who is to come. Moreover, as a human person is who he is in virtue not only of his relation to man and nature, but also of his relation to the god he worships (see below, ch. III, sect. 3), so an historical community is defined not only by its position in time and space, but by the object of its devotion. Thus we may say that the faith and expectations of all significant human com-

---

[3] Augustine, *De Civitate Dei*, XIX, 24: a society is "a group of reasonable beings united among themselves by a love having the same object."

munities have at least implicitly some sort of transcendent reference, i.e., they have their gods, and that the church is distinguished because it places its faith in the true God, known to it in Jesus Christ (cf. Eph 2:12). This it is which shapes and molds, or determines, its being as an historical community.

3) On the other hand, the church is what it is, i.e., it has this concrete character, because its adoration, its faith, hope, and love are directed toward the God who has already acted decisively toward it.[4] Its being is unequivocally a response to what is absolutely prior to all human response. This is the true sense in which the life or being of the church is lodged beyond itself.[5] Not as if there were some invisible "real form" or "essence," planted out by God, which the humanly visible community reflects. Rather the church exists in movement; this is of its very being (it is noteworthy how many of the New Testament images for the Christian and the church suggest the movement of coming from and going to God in Christ[6]). The church

[4] Here is the point at which we must pass beyond what theology and sociology can say in common with respect to the church. Faith alone is assured that the belief, worship and obedience of the church is in fact a response to the divine act. This is the truth in the epistemological interpretation of the polarity of the church (see ch. I, sect. 2, *d*).

[5] The argument of this paragraph is in itself incomplete, and requires to be filled out in relation to the nature of the church as eschatological community (see ch. IV).

[6] The word *ecclesia* certainly suggests this, in its reference to God's "calling out" the community. Especially pertinent images include: the way, ambassadors (II Cor 5:20), living sacrifice, the aroma of Christ (II Cor 2:15), access to God, exiles (I Peter 1:1; 2:1), colony of heaven (Phil 3:20), of God and born of God (I Jn 4–5), priesthood (I Peter 2:5, 9), the elect, the called, the chosen (Rom 8:30, 33; I Cor 1:26; I Thess 1:4;

as social and historical movement is at the same time movement toward God, which is itself utterly dependent upon the movement of God to man. It can be said that the church *exists* just in this relation. As humanly concrete community, it depends wholly upon the act of God who has called it into being in Jesus Christ and whose continued turning toward the church alone makes possible its turning to him. The faith and love of the church toward God is entirely grounded in, called forth and embraced by the gracious action of God. Its determination of itself rests in God's prior determination. Thus the church, without ceasing to be genuinely human, social, and historical reality, has its existence in God. Those who were no people have become a people by this calling, forgiving and glorifying. Like the people of the old covenant, this people is constituted by a covenant, and has its existence in that dynamic relation. Also like the people of the old covenant, this people has an incriminating history of disobedience and faithlessness, but even its faithlessness can be understood only in relation to God, and testifies both to its reality as human community and to its entire dependence on him. Thus the church is what it is, the people of God, both because of what it is "in itself" and because of the creative and redemptive activity of God which makes it to be.

This polarity of the church's being is most clearly seen

I Peter 2:9). Also relevant, of course, is the eschatological characterization of the community: the church moves toward and already participates in the new age; it comes from Christ and it goes to meet him. Another dimension of the church's movement toward God is suggested by the metaphors of growth (e.g., Eph 2:21).

as we view the church as worshipping community. Here is the center of the church's life—namely, the continual gathering of the community in common worship. That means not only the assembling for the preaching of the Word and the celebration of the sacraments, though these acts are primary in the church's worship, but also whenever two or three are gathered in Christ's name in praise, thanksgiving, confession, petition and intercession. The whole movement, structure and being of the community in relation to the historic Person, who is the living Lord, is here (and here most visibly before the world) brought to focus. And this assembling takes place in response to the electing will of God; it is a covenant response which occurs within God's establishment of the covenant with his people, a self-determination in obedience to and acceptance of the divine determination.

The central point may also be expressed in terms of love, of *koinonia* as fellowship in the church. These terms refer to a quite concrete, manifest quality of the common life, to a definite kind of relation among persons. It is inconceivable, from the perspective of the New Testament, to think of love of the neighbor apart from visible expression in human existence. This love is the uniting of men in one body, the breaking down of social differentiations. It is the more excellent way, the test of the presence of the Spirit and the mind of Christ. Love of the neighbor is a determinative mark of the social and historical life of the people.

But love of the neighbor is grounded in love of God.

The direction of life toward a human other depends upon the direction of life toward the divine Other. The immanent historical relation is inseparable from the relation to the transcendent. And both love of neighbor and love of God depend on God's love of self and neighbor. None of these relations exists without the other, yet there is an order of priority and determination. The love which is shed abroad in our hearts is the working of the Spirit. The act of God and the act of man are not dissolved into one another, yet the act of the human self is embraced by the divine act. Human love of the neighbor and of God depends upon the love which comes to man in the humanity of Jesus Christ (therefore in and through temporal process), which is also the eternal faithfulness of God in his love. Thus the love which is in the church, without ceasing to be the act of the community in time and space, is a being of the church in the love of God. Or, to put it in proper order, the creative and redemptive activity of God's love calls into existence a people responding in love, in which the working of God issues in creaturely social and historical community. The being, the ontology, of the church in humanly social and historical process is not in contradiction to, or extraneous to, but wholly conjoined to its being in God, for its existence *qua* such community depends upon its being held by his love and united in its common love for him.

Chapter III

THE FORM OF THE SERVANT

I. IN THE COMMUNITY

IN THE previous chapter we began to delineate certain features of the ontology of the church. The church is a community in time and space, a *congregatio* whose self-existence quite resembles that of other human communities, both in its sociality and its temporality. Yet just in this creaturely historical being the church depends wholly upon the activity of God; it is the *convocatio*, whose being a people is constituted by a being *called*. This dependence, this existence of the church in God's act, was described both as the determination of the creative memory, hope and loyalty of the community through the historical event of Jesus Christ, and as the continuous act of God in grace and love, to which the unifying faith and love of the church are a response.

Still a further specification of the church's being, both as a humanly historical people and as a working of God, and particularly of the way these come together, must now be added. When we describe the church as necessarily a social and historical reality, whose life is expressed in the

74

familiar dynamics of social process and communal existence in time, we are not making an external and *a priori* judgment as to what the church must be. We do not say that, because all human communities have a certain character, the church must also conform to this pattern. Rather, viewing the church from within, we confess that it is such because God does not scorn to meet us in the history in which we live. Whatever necessity is here derives simply from what God has done. This is the way God has acted. As he has chosen "what is foolish in the world to shame the wise" and "what is weak in the world to shame the strong" (I Cor 1:27), he has not hesitated to give this treasure into earthen vessels (II Cor 4:7), i.e., into everyday pottery. In the establishment of his people, he has not translated its members into a heavenly sphere, nor planted in the midst of humanity a wholly alien community,[1] whose patterns are simply foreign to the world which surrounds it. No, he has humbled himself, choosing to establish community with us in the midst of our humanity and weakness.

To put it in other language, the Holy Spirit is not only free to judge and to remain transcendent over all human forms and formulations, but free to bind himself to the concrete, to use precisely the fragile vessels, the workaday pots of our historical forms. God does not choose to redeem history apart from history, nor create new com-

---

[1] We are strangers and aliens, yes, and a colony of heaven, but strangers to the "world" in the sense of the present aeon, the realm of bondage to sin, and not strangers to human community. Moreover, our strangeness to the world cannot be stated apart from our hope, the fact that we exist not only as called and already sons but as those who await.

munity apart from human community. The Spirit works in and by means of flesh and time and human togetherness.

Nowhere is this more clearly seen, perhaps, than in the life of the Israel of the old covenant, in God's long and patient preparation for the coming of the incarnate Word. The very human vessel Israel is forged not simply in the majesty of divine promise and command on a mountain top, but in a common experience of suffering and flight and battle. The unity of covenant is intermingled with unities of family, tribe and nation. The victory of Yahweh over Baal is at the same time national triumph and freedom. The adoration of the Lord of history springs from the background of a nomadic people and the historical circumstances of a tiny nation. The divine kingship is symbolized (for a time) in human kingship. The hope for the Day of the Lord grows out of repeated political disaster. Prophetic judgment can reflect not only the memory of the ancient faith but also the protest of agrarian and seminomadic life against a new commercial culture. The understanding of the divine will for human relations develops in the context of the communal experience.[2]

In such aspects as these, and they are only random examples, one thing at least becomes quite clear: God is not in the least afraid to achieve his ends precisely in and through

[2] The point here is not in the least to describe Israel and its faith in evolutionary or any other particular scheme of development. Such questions as the precise scope of the Mosaic faith, the point of appearance of an explicit or implicit monotheism, and the extent to which the prophets either maintained or developed the received faith, etc., are irrelevant to the argument here.

all manner of historical development. The life and faith of Israel are not created *de novo* and without relation to the world of the ancient Near East. God calls his people into being in the midst of and through that world. The forms of Israel's life include in themselves (and not only as sin) religious and social forms of contemporary cultures. Israel's thought takes up categories of an ancient Semitic Near East, and we can probe their meaning only in relation (both of difference and likeness) to the thought of that world.

The theological significance of this is just its testimony to the condescension and lowliness of God in his relation to man and to the whole of his creation, and if this is true of the life of Israel it is equally true of the church's life. It is true of the scriptures, in which we are met not with a new divine language, but with quite familiar human languages, with thought forms, images and expressions drawn from quite definite cultural contexts; and if we wish to hear the Word of God in the scriptures, we shall do it only as we attend to these human words and images, and indeed as we see them in all their interconnections both within the Bible and in the thought-contexts from which they come. It is true of Baptism, which we are able to see not only in relation to our Lord's baptism and his command, but also in the context of Jewish washing and circumcision and of the initiation rites of Hellenistic mystery cults. It is true of the Eucharist, which may well have connections both with the Passover meal and a variety of cult sacrificial meals. It is true of the development of the ministry in the church, in all its resemblances to other institutional patterns. And it is true of every creed and confession of the church, where the witness of faith is expressed in the fragile language and categories of succeeding times.[3]

All these features of the church's life are to be seen as signs of the way God, in his infinite graciousness, adapts himself to the forms of our history. Now in saying this, we are not to suppose that the activity of God is reduced to the immanent processes of history. For the aim of this gracious humbling is God's own transcendent purpose. He takes our brokenness in order to heal, and his work of condescension does not leave things just as they were. He enters history in order to transform. But we must not hasten on to speak of that transformation until we have acknowledged the fullness of condescension, just as we cannot speak of resurrection and ascension apart from incarnation and crucifixion.[4]

At the moment, the crucial thing is to see that the whole life of the church is testimony to God's gracious willingness to establish community with us in our humanity and our history. Negatively, this means that the reality of the church as the people of God is not to be established or defended by denying its involvement in human culture. Positively, this shows the fullness of God's condescension.[5]

[3] We may also think of the possible relation of the primitive church to the community of the Qumran texts.

[4] Of course, we are really dealing here with interrelated and inseparable matters, but I think there is value in the order of thought here being followed.

[5] Lionel Thornton makes the point well in *Revelation and the Modern World*, London, A. & C. Black, Ltd., pp. 5f.: "If there is 'mastery' in

And if we take this seriously, we have to say that it concerns not only the great symbols of the church—scripture, sacraments, creeds, ministry—every aspect of its life may manifest the same pattern of his working. The mind of Christ can be operative not only in the church council gathered to pronounce decision on great doctrines of the

---

God's modes of action towards the order within which he manifests himself, it is all of one piece with the action of Jesus Christ when he took a towel and girded himself to wash the disciples' feet . . . the divine action adapted itself to, and even identified itself with, the given forms of history in order that by so doing it might transform their spiritual significance. The possibility of an explanation which sees the biblical religion as a product of its environment is due precisely to the fact that the divine action is perfectly adjusted to that environment, and that in all its manifold aspects. The fact that at almost any stage of history the religion of Israel, and not less the religion of the apostolic church, can seem explicable in terms of contemporary culture-forms, so far from militating against the truth of Christianity, bears witness to the completeness of the divine condescension. God's self-identification with the minutiae of contemporary life and thought is all of one piece with the doctrine of incarnation."

This perspective seems to me of profound value for our understanding of revelation, as well as for the life of the church in general. Difficulties, however, arise at at least two points in Thornton's development. First, the way in which, throughout this volume and its sequels, he develops the corollaries regarding the importance of *all* the scriptural details. Second, more generally, and fundamental to the first, his understanding of what is meant by the transformation of the forms of history. Here he seems to me not only to use the pattern of incarnation to illumine God's work in the church and in the world, but ultimately to absorb the church in the incarnation. I.e., he sees not only analogy or congruity between the person of Christ and the nature of the church, but really identity of nature. I should hold, rather, that no more than analogy is possible, and this precisely because of sin in the church. The transformation of the church must be viewed under the rubric of eschatology in a way which distinguishes it fundamentally from the transformation of humanity in the person of Christ. See chs. IV, V and VII. Obviously, this has important implications also for the doctrine of the sacraments and the ministry.

church, but in the board of trustees met to discuss the care of church property. The voice of Christ may be heard not only in the theological discourse of the minister, but in the legal or commercial or rural language of the congregation. And surely the pattern of God's lowliness is to be discerned in the mission of the church to the unbeliever, in its concern with the ordering of society, and in its ministry to every human need, as well as in the liturgy, confession and polity of the church.

Moreover, the condescension of God means that he is willing to take real chances, and the way is open for corruption and sin in the church. That the church is called to be human society means that the church is liable to the perversions of national, racial and class division. That God works through the church as human fellowship means that it can become merely an agency for warmth of companionship, for humanitarianism and for emotional release, with a minimum of demands upon its membership. That God allows the church to be an intricate institution with business concerns means that it can become a reflection of typical business interests in survival, in reports, in sales, and in customer or stockholder satisfaction. That the children of God are in the church a family involves the hazard that it may absorb into itself instabilities of contemporary family life.[6] But God is willing to take all these risks, as the whole history of the church makes amply clear.

[6] Cf. the analysis by Warren Ashby in "Caste and Class in the Local Church: Relations with the Institutional Environment," prepared as a study paper for the North American Conference on Faith and Order, 1957, subsequently published in *Christian Unity in North America*, J. R. Nelson, ed., Bethany Press, 1958.

Finally, it must be emphasized that it is *God* who is the subject of this gracious humbling. We are not to speak of the church as adapting and conforming itself to the patterns of human society as if the church itself were some entity essentially above all this poor history and humanity.[7] On the contrary, the church is that lowly humanity and history to which and in which God condescends to be present in Jesus Christ, calling it to be and by his Spirit working in it the new humanity which is at the same time true humanity.

2. IN THE INCARNATION

When we describe the pattern of divine action in the church by such words as condescension and humbling, we obviously have in mind also the manner of God's coming in Jesus Christ. This is the decisive coming through which all the rest is to be understood. God's work in the church is all of a piece with the incarnation; his use of the weak vessels of our community is intelligible in the light of his assumption of humanity in Jesus Christ. We are not allowed simply to equate the presence of God in the church with his being in Christ. The church is not itself an incarnation or an extension of the incarnation. (The reasons for this judgment will become clearer as we proceed.) Yet the being of the church is analogous, or congruous, with the person of its Lord.

The lowliness of God's coming in Christ confronts us at

[7] Versus, e.g., the viewpoint of M. J. Congar, *Divided Christendom*, p. 89. This way of thinking is especially common in Roman Catholic theology.

the outset in the enigma of Jesus' life and self-presentation. There is an ambiguity and hiddenness about his whole career. His words are full of the glory of the kingdom and its nearness, but the words are those of a carpenter's son and wandering rabbi. He claims that the promise of the prophet is fulfilled, but nothing seems fundamentally altered. His words about himself are at best unclear, and perhaps a hopeless puzzle. Even his closest followers often understand him badly. His claims to authority have no evident certification, for his form is that of a servant. His deeds no less than his words testify to the enigma of his person, and at the last he is impotent before his opponents.

This is a familiar point, which we have already touched on (see ch. I), and there is no need to labor it. We are well aware that only in faith is Jesus of Nazareth apprehended to be the Christ, the Son of God. The question remains, however, as to what it is that faith apprehends. Does faith see in the figure of Jesus Christ a majesty and authority which is overlooked by the eye of ordinary man; that is, does faith see something else than unbelief sees? Or does faith see the same figure in a different light, viz., that just this visible figure is the presence of God? To pose the alternative more properly: does faith affirm Jesus to be the Christ *in spite of* the human form and weakness, or precisely *in it* and *because* of it? There are senses in which both of the former questions have to be answered in the affirmative. But certainly with respect to the latter statement of the alternative, the judgment of faith is clear. Jesus is the Son of God not in spite of the historical form of his humanity, but exactly *in it*. Just this historical figure is the veritable presence of the Lord of heaven and earth. The form which hides is at the same time the form of revelation. The reality of incarnation is not to be observed at this point or that point in contrast to other points in Jesus' career, but precisely in the whole of the career, which in its totality is the witness to the presence of God. Thus in the gospel of Mark, the explicit Christological affirmation comes only at the end of the drama; when Jesus has died and the curtain of the temple is torn in two, the confession is made in the words of the centurion that "truly this man was a son of God" (Mk 15:39). And in the gospels generally, the claim is expressed primarily in dramatic and dynamic form, in the whole story of the life from birth to resurrection.[1] And it must be so given, for only in that wholeness is the form of God's presence to be discerned.

What this means is that in Jesus Christ faith learns what lordship truly is and what true humanity is.[2] Faith does not

---

[1] Prof. James Barr makes this point, especially in relation to the gospel of Mark, in illuminating fashion in "Christ in Gospel and Creed," *Scottish Journal of Theology*, VIII, 1955, pp. 225ff.

[2] This does not mean that we either can or do derive our understanding of what God is and what man is simply (as it were deductively) from the biblical witness to Jesus Christ. It is, of course, a grave error to force the biblical witness into the mold of preconceived notions of the nature of God and man. *A priori* conceptions of deity and humanity have worked havoc in Christian theology, and nowhere more than in Christology. But it is also wrong to suppose that we can approach the problem of incarnation with empty minds, deducing everything from the witness to Jesus Christ. This can lead to the equally great danger of concealing from ourselves the notions which we bring and introducing them surreptitiously into theology.

A proper theological procedure is more dialectical than either of these alternatives, moving back and forth continuously between the

discern the divinity of Jesus Christ in some contra-human aspects of his career, which are hidden behind or interspersed with the moments of his humanity, but it sees just this humility and weakness as the form of his true divinity. He has taken the form of a servant, a human form, has humbled himself and become obedient to death, even the death on a cross, and *therefore* God has highly exalted him and bestowed on him the name above every name (Phil 2:7–9). His lordship does not lie in his "majesty," but in his obedience, i.e., in his humiliation. It lies in the lowly manner of his coming and living among men. It lies in his coming not to be ministered unto but to minister. It lies in his taking a towel and girding himself to wash his disciples' feet. It lies in his claiming all for God, and his subjection of his will entirely to that of the Father. It lies in his submitting to baptism at the hands of John. It lies in his entire life of sacrificing himself in love. It lies in the same way even in his mighty works of healing, which Matthew puts under the rubric of his suffering, fulfilling the word of the prophet that he should take our infirmities and bear our diseases (Mt 8:16–17).[3] And this power and

poles of the revelation in Jesus Christ and our particular human situation, with all its categories and perspectives. The conceptions of God and man which we bring to Jesus Christ must indeed be laid at his feet, crucified and transformed in the light of the incarnation; but the incarnation is itself inevitably understood in the light of our historical perspective, and must be so interpreted if the gospel is to be truly proclaimed (for a more general statement of this view, in terms of the relation of theology and culture, cf. J. Dillenberger and C. Welch, *Protestant Christianity*, ch. XIV, esp. pp. 323ff.).

[3] I am indebted to my colleague, Prof. Paul Meyer, for pointing out this connection.

lordship lies in his final condescension in the baptism of
blood, in taking death upon himself.

With right, Karl Barth in his doctrine of reconciliation
has reversed the common identification of Christ's Godhead with his exaltation and his humanity with his humiliation. The lordship of Christ is exhibited in his identification with sinful man, particularly with the disobedient Son
Israel. Herein is revealed the heart of God's grace and love,
which is his being God. And as his self-humiliation is an
act of God's love, it is a possibility of his being, and not
a contradiction but the true disclosure of his omnipotence,
omniscience and glory.[4]

Just at this point we may discern some outlines of the
analogy of Christ and the church. The humanity of Christ

---

[4] Cf. *KD*, IV/1, pp. 83ff., 171ff.

From this perspective, we are better able to state the point of the
doctrine of the *communicatio idiomatum*, especially as it means more
than the mere ascription to the humanity of properties properly belonging to deity and *vice versa*. We are not left simply with the alternative of conceiving the humanity of Christ as informed by God's being
in the sense of impassibility, omnipotence and omniscience (in the
ancient Christological controversies, it was not really supposed that the
Word was truly characterized by the limitation and suffering of the
humanity; the *communicatio* was largely one-way), with all the questions that this raises about its remaining real humanity; *or* of viewing
the two natures of Christ as somehow existing simply in parallel to each
other. Instead, we are able to say that in the most ultimate sense, the
being of God is given in the humanity, or that this humanity has been
given the property of deity. The babe in the arms of Mary does indeed
hold in his hand the globe of the world, because the power and glory
of God are revealed just in the weakness of the infant. This is, to be
sure, not all that needs to be said about the unity of God and man in
Christ, but it is a necessary thing to say. It also means thinking together
the notion of *communicatio idiomatum* with the more active and
soteriological concept of *communicatio operationum*.

is seen not as obstacle but as the sphere of God's presence. The form of man and of identification with sinful man is truly the form of God's being in Christ. And the servant pattern relates to the being of the church both as statement and as command; the way of God in Christ illumines his way with the church in this double sense. As he humbles himself to assume manhood in Christ, so he creates the community of Christ in the midst of and in the form of our humanity. And as he is in Christ the concrete servant of men, taking into himself the infirmity and disease of mankind and being obedient unto death, so the church is commanded to follow in the way of self-denial and crucifixion. As the humanity of the church is one with the humanity of its Lord, so the pattern of its humanity is to be conformed to the form of his. It is sent out into the world as a suffering servant.

The lordship of Christ cannot, of course, be defined simply in terms of humiliation. Humiliation and exaltation belong together. As the prologue to the Fourth Gospel makes clear, it is the Word in the fullness of creative (and reconciling and redeeming) being, through whom all things are made, who became flesh and dwelt among us, full of grace and truth. The two sides must be held together in simultaneity. The lordship of Christ is defined not only by the lowliness of birth and crucifixion, but by resurrection and ascension. And only from the standpoint of resurrection is faith able to make its proper judgment about the form of the servant. We must be careful not to misstate the matter. The resurrection speaks both of the manhood and the

Godhood of Jesus Christ. It is the exaltation of the same manhood which suffered and died, and it is the manifestation that the divine power of condescension is the ultimate power, even over death, therefore the almightiness of the creator himself. Just because of this, faith is unable to view the presence of God in Christ as simply identical with his humanity. The statement of Chalcedon is here a necessary boundary: if the divine and the human natures are *inseparabiliter*, they are also *inconfuse*. Faith does not see now the humanity of Christ, now his Godhead, as if men are first attracted to Jesus the man and then apprehend his lordship, or as if the features of his life are to be parceled out to humanity and divinity respectively.[5] The claim of

---

[5] A few sentences from the Tome of Leo may be cited as typical of the persistent tendency so to distinguish divine and human features of the life of Christ: "To feel hunger, thirst, and weariness, and to sleep, is evidently human; but to satisfy thousands of men with five loaves, and to bestow living water on the Samaritan woman, the drinking of which would cause her who drank it to thirst no more; to walk on the surface of the sea with feet which did not sink, and to allay the 'rising billows' by rebuking the tempest is without doubt Divine. As then, to omit many other examples, it does not belong to the same nature to weep in an emotion of pity for a dead friend, and to raise that same friend from the dead with a word of power, after the stone over the tomb where he had been for four days buried had been removed; or to hang on the wood and, changing the light into darkness to make all the elements tremble; or, to be pierced with nails and to open the gates of Paradise to the faith of the robber; so it does not belong to the same nature to say, 'I and the Father are One,' and 'the Father is greater than I.' For although in the Lord Jesus Christ there is One Person of God and man, yet that whence the suffering is common to both is one thing, and that whence the glory common to both is another." (tr. by T. H. Bindley, in *The Oecumenical Documents of the Faith*, 4th ed., London, Methuen & Co., Ltd., pp. 227f.)

Leo's insistence on the reality of both the human and the divine natures, which is evident here, of course compels our assent. But this

God is always present with and in the claim of man. Yet these are not identified or equated. Viewing from the perspective of the resurrection, faith sees the mystery of the divine presence in and through the humanity. The gospels see it as there from the beginning in the story of the birth in weakness, yet attended by the adoration of shepherds and wise men. It is there at the end, in the confession of the centurion at the moment of Jesus' death. And the divine claim is present throughout his personal existence and authority and message, which bespeak not only the authority of men but of God.

In other words, that the form of God's being in Christ is the form of a servant does not negate its being the presence of the One who is the creator and lord of the universe. It does not allow us to escape what we may call the ontological problem of the incarnation; the meaning of humanity and Godhead in Christ, and their unity. It does, however, require us to approach this question first and fundamentally with reference to the historical figure of the incarnate Lord. For it is the historical figure to which the attention of men is drawn, and which becomes for faith both testimony and form truly expressive of God.[6] Precisely from this we are to learn what it means to speak of the essential humanity and deity of Jesus Christ, there-

___

way of speaking both restricts the presence of God in Christ to certain aspects of the historical career, and reveals clearly the inadequate (because unbiblical) conception of deity which infected so much of the ancient (and not only ancient) Christological discussion.

[6] This significance of the historical figure requires us to take another look at the easy and widespread rejection of the "quest for the historical Jesus." See Additional Note A, at the end of this chapter.

fore what the true meaning of humanity and deity is. And because it is in human form that the Son of God is found, it is at least permissible to begin by inquiring what sort of humanity is presented in Jesus of Nazareth, though remembering always that the claim of his humanity is not to be divided from the claim of the Word who was made flesh in him.

3. THE MANHOOD OF THE SERVANT

When we turn to the New Testament with the question of how the humanity of this historical figure is depicted, we are required to change, or at least to broaden, our customary perspectives. For the New Testament (and the Old Testament as well) is not concerned with human existence simply under the rubrics of bodily existence, finite limitations, etc., but equally and perhaps more fundamentally with man as participant in a socio-historical stream and as related to God. Human nature is a very concrete and distinctive sort of existence.[1]

---

[1] For this reason, we may wonder whether the term "nature," as used in the affirmation that Jesus Christ possessed both a complete human nature and a complete divine nature, is not for us misleading or at least restrictive in its connotations. The problem is not at all that the words *natura* and *physis* are "philosophical" terms—I have not the slightest interest here in posing a contradiction between "Greek" and "Hebrew" categories—but that they are in themselves such colorless terms, and may suggest non-concrete and even impersonal categories for humanity. And while we must fully respect the intention of the Fathers to include in the phrase "human nature" everything that goes to make up essential human existence, we may suspect that even they at times were led by it to think primarily of humanity in terms of man's relation to the world of "nature," even when they spoke of soul and mind as well as flesh and blood.

To be sure, the New Testament is insistent that the Word became *flesh*, that the humanity of Jesus Christ was the reality of man in and before nature, in the finitude of time and space. And this is of signal importance. Jesus was a man with a genuine human body. He is born, hungers, thirsts, is weary, sleeps, suffers and dies. His emotions are genuinely human emotions. His mind is a human mind, with the limitations of finite subjectivity. He learns as men learn (Lk 2:46, 47, 52). He disclaims omniscience (Mk 13:32).[2] His consciousness is a truly human consciousness, his psychology that of human personality. His knowledge of God, the awareness of God's presence and love, is a human awareness, we must even say religious experience. His faith and obedience, his sinlessness, is the perfection of *humanity*. More particularly, he shares as man in the perspectives and categories of a given time and place, as an historically conditioned person. He is a Jew of the first century (not a Greek philosopher or a 20th century European), and to deny this either by implication or silence is to make nonsense of our faith in God's preparation for the coming of the Messiah through the history of Israel. The existence of Jesus as a man in this particular historical situation, with all that that implies by way of limitation and conditioning, is not something merely to be admitted in passing, but to be insisted upon as central to our view of the incarnation.

[2] I cannot but consider interpretations like that of E. L. Mascall (cf. *Christ, the Christian, and the Church*, pp. 57ff.) as attempts to explain away the manifest meaning of the text in the interest of, as it seems to me, a grossly defective Christology.

But such assertions as these, essential as they are, are not sufficient to encompass the picture of the humanity of Jesus which the New Testament presents. The distinctive, even crucial features of the biblical portrait of human existence are expressed in more dynamic terms. The emphasis is always on man in relation to other men and to God. It is man in sin and obedience, man in the "flesh" or in the Spirit, who holds the center of attention. And what is crucial about the humanity of Jesus is that he is the Anointed One, the Messiah of God, and the first-born of brethren in the church. His is the New Humanity, the humanity of the Second Adam.

This gives us an important clue, I think, to a more adequate understanding of what truly constitutes humanity. Man is man, not only as part of and over against nature, but man in relation to society and to God. And this being-in-relation is not merely accidental to his being, or simply a reference to the "meaning" of his selfhood, but constitutive of his *being man*. He exists only in this way. This is the nature of his personal existence.

On the one side, man exists *qua* man only in and before society. He is defined by the people to which he belongs. He is never man in general, but always man of a particular race, nationality, culture, family, etc. He is inescapably social man, and this means not only that he needs society, but that he is formed and exists in a matrix of social relations. From our contemporary understanding of the formation of personality, we are able to see how fundamentally true this is. Personality cannot be formed except in and as part of a network of personal relations, so we can say that social environment determines personal existence. This does not mean exclusive determination. Individuality is not dissolved; personality is not just a point in a field of social relations. The term is not swallowed up in the relation. It is the self which is related, and which becomes a self in reaction to as well as in conformity with these relations.[3] Nevertheless, the self would not be itself apart from its relation to other selves. And just in self-awareness and decision is the self most truly social.

In other words, I am what and who I am precisely in my involvement in community and history. I am not myself apart from being a son, a husband, a father, a teacher, a friend, etc. I am not myself except in relations to the many communities of which I am a part, political, economic, social, religious—in whose memories and hopes I share and by which I am shaped. That is, my being man, having a human nature, is defined at least as much by the fact that I exist in a particular complex of social relations as it is by my having a body and certain psychological and mental capacities and limitations.

Such considerations as these are useful, and perhaps indispensable, to our understanding of the biblical concern

---

[3] Thus once achieved, selfhood can be maintained, for a time at least, in complete isolation from human contacts. It should be remarked that I am not trying to state a complete theory of the human self. The argument here does not depend on a final resolution of the problem of selfhood and personal identity in relation to social environment. It does require rejection of complete social determinism, but beyond that only the recognition that personal existence is inseparable from the being of a self in relation.

with humanity, and in particular its conception of the solidarity of the people and of the humanity of Jesus Christ. The humanity of Christ is his being man among men and for men. It includes the relation in which he exists with the people of Israel and the community of his followers. We may think, e.g., of the remarkable number of New Testament names and titles for Jesus, in which he is designated in explicit terms of social relations: he is rabbi, teacher, master, servant, son of Joseph, of Mary, king, judge, root and offspring of David, bridegroom, shepherd, pioneer, high priest, first-born, the last Adam.[4] The humanity of Jesus means his having come in the midst of the people of Israel and his being the first-born of brethren. Moreover, it means the very concrete self-giving of himself in love for men, in receiving all unto himself, in humbling himself to serve them in their need and in dying for them. The form of the servant is not only the form of divine condescension, but the designation of the humanity of Jesus Christ. Here, also, we must say that humanity is not merely flesh and psychological endowment, but man in relation to man. The being of Christ as man is not only structured but constituted by his being a man for men, one who refuses to be an individual apart and insists on identifying himself with others.

This insight into the social dimension of human nature does not carry all the way to an appreciation of the biblical

[4] A further feature of many of these terms, and of the NT names for Jesus generally, is the impossibility of saying that one refers purely to the humanity of Jesus and another to his divinity. Both references are often inseparably present.

view of the solidarity of humanity, or of the unity of the humanity of Christ with his people. The biblical notion of the community seems to go even further. Israel is one in the covenant; Israel's sin is always the guilt and sin of the people; the church is the body of Christ; Christ embodies the people in himself in temptation and in suffering; his acts are his own personal acts and at the same time corporate acts. This is a matter which must be discussed further when we come to speak of "participation" (ch. V), but we may be helped by looking at another essential dimension of humanity.

Man is theological man as well as social man and natural man. Now this is not simply a way of saying that man is a worshipping animal, who if he does not know any gods will soon create one. It is rather a statement of what is, from the perspective of Christian faith, the deepest level of human existence. Man as the creature of God exists, he has his being, in relation to God. His being "in himself," which is an aspect of his creaturely existence, is never apart from his being related to God, whether in obedience or sin, acceptance or refusal. Again, this is no accidental feature of human existence; it is the decisive determination of humanity. In his deepest selfhood, to the core of his being, man exists in relation to God. He cannot withdraw from this relation, as he can from society, because he is here not related to finite selves but to the ultimate ground of his being. He may be rebellious and deformed humanity, he may seek to deny his dependence and refuse his love to the Creator, but his very movement of disobedience and distrust takes place within the structure of this ontological relation.

But it must also be said that man is made *for God*. Here too his humanity is to be understood in terms of movement and process which affect the fibre of his selfhood. In this sense his personal existence is a becoming, either of true humanity and personality in acknowledgment and love of God, of acceptance of his actual state, or of distorted and impoverished humanity. Thus his existence is a sphere of tension and conflict, of the body of sin and the body of redemption, of the struggle between the power of God and the powers of darkness.

In this sphere we find the culmination of New Testament concern with the humanity of Christ. He is man precisely because he has entered into this realm of struggle, of temptation and doubt. In him the conflict between God and the devil is waged. "In the days of his flesh," as Hebrews puts it, "Jesus offered up prayers and supplications, with loud cries and tears, to him who was able to save him from death, and he was heard for his godly fear" (Heb 5:7). He comes into the very situation of human sin,[5] yet as the obedient Son who learning obedience is made perfect. Central to this picture is the reality of movement, of wrestling and achievement, of victory won. This is essential not only to the concept in Hebrews of learning obedience through suffering, but to the Pauline portrait of the victory over the powers of evil (a victory won not on

[5] See ch. V, sect. 2.

the cross alone, but on the cross as the culmination of the entire life), and especially to the whole presentation in the gospels, in which the being of this person is a being directed toward an end, a life formed by movement toward culmination. The New Testament is throughout concerned with the "movement" of Christ's life—his birth, life, teaching, death, resurrection, ascension and return (for in his ascended power he remains true man). This pattern is also expressed in Irenaeus' term "recapitulation," which sees the humanity of Jesus not in static terms but in terms of moving and dynamic fulfillment.

Moreover, just in the forging of this personhood, we see the creation of the new humanity, which is true humanity (not in the sense of transition from incomplete to complete, or from less to more human, but as the bringing of true humanity to full expression in the whole of the process). The true humanity of Jesus consists in his being from first to last the man before God and for God. All that he does and is, is in relation to God. His being is a being of love for God, for the transcendent power and good alone worthy of adoration. His hope is entirely in God and for God. His obedience is directed explicitly to the One who is Father and Creator. His humility and his faith are absolute dependence and trust in God alone. And his faith is never something in itself, but entirely a relation to God.[6] All this stands at the center of his exist-

---

[6] Cf. the remarkable Christological statement in terms of the "virtues" of Jesus as love, hope, obedience, faith and humility, in H. R. Niebuhr, *Christ and Culture*, pp. 14–29.

ence as man. His humanity is constituted finally and supremely by his being both man for man and man for God.[7]

Yet precisely here, in the entirety of Jesus' being for man and for God, we see him also as the being of God for man. His love for God, which is the love with which men are called to love God, is the love of one who is truly the Son of God. His love for man is the love of God for man. As man in his being wholly directed toward God, he is at the same time one with the Father in relation to men.[8] One might be tempted to put this in language reminiscent of Schleiermacher, saying that Jesus is so filled with God as the object of his faith, humility, love, obedience and hope, that this is truly the presence of God in him. That would be wrong. But it can and must be said that this is both a sign and a point of the unity of God and man in him. That God is so entirely the object of his person is a sign of the being of God in him, and at the same time a locus of his mediatorship, i.e., his existence at the center of the movement from God to man and from man to God.

4. THE UNITY OF THE PERSON

If, then, we are able to understand the fullness of the humanity of Jesus Christ through the depth of his exist-

[7] Just at the point, of the being of humanity in relation to God, we may be helped in understanding the solidarity or "corporateness" of humanity. We are united not only by the social nature of our selves, but as in this togetherness we stand in relation to God, fundamentally determined by our participation in one another in obedience and acceptance and/or in rejection and deformity. And our unity in this relation is defined not only from our side, but from the side of God's movement toward us. (see ch. V, sect. 3)

[8] Cf. H. R. Niebuhr, *Christ and Culture*, p. 29.

ence in relation to God, we are helped in the attempt to speak of the unity of his person, particularly as looked at from the manward side. As true humanity, constituted as such by its being directed wholly toward God and utterly dependent on him, the manhood of Jesus Christ is the appropriate and adequate organ for the presence of the Eternal Word and the expression of his purposes.

But this unity needs to be viewed also from the Godward side—and this is the primary side, for it was not a man who assumed divinity, but God who assumed humanity, and nothing we say can be allowed to obscure or qualify the primacy of the self-movement of God in the incarnation. Here too one must think in the first instance of the *act* of God, of God's being in relation to man and the world in Jesus Christ. For here we are able to speak most unambiguously of the unity of Christ's person, from the side of God's being present to men in Christ. Christ's being of love for men—and this refers not only to his explicit servitude and humility and suffering for men, but equally to the authority and majesty of his presence—is God's being present in love for men. We are not concerned with two different and separable loves, a human love and a divine love, but one love. The love of Christ for man, which is the fullness of his humanity, expresses precisely the love of God for man, veritably God's loving of men in this human loving and giving and dying. These cannot be split apart. The movement of Jesus' love is one with the humiliation and condescension of God.[1] The act of God in Christ is the pres-

[1] We may recall here the difficulty of assigning the NT titles for Jesus,

ence of God; i.e., God's presence in Christ is the act of this life.

That is why, we may suggest, the Christology of the gospels is not presented in formal assertions about the being of Christ but in the story of his life. This is not a defect to be remedied by later generations, an inadequate Christology to be replaced by a "proper" doctrine. On the contrary, it is an essential form of Christological statement, because it conforms to the way in which God is present in Christ, viz., in dynamic act moving through the whole of the life from birth to resurrection. In this way, the person and the work of Christ are not split apart, but held properly together. For person and work are here one; Christ's being who he is, is the same as what he does, i.e., the movement of his life in unity at once with men and with God. Christ's being is his being sent, God acting in him and his living in complete dependence on God. His being God and man is a being in time, i.e., the act of reconciling through life, death and resurrection.

From this perspective it is possible to appreciate the significance of the Antiochene attempt to deal with the question of the unity of Christ's person, while insisting on the reality of both the divinity and humanity. The inadequacy of their descriptions of the unity—as an indwelling by divine goodwill, or unity of disposition of will; or according to love, or union of title, will, energy, authority,

---

especially those explicitly referring to his relation to the community, either his humanity or his deity. They cannot be simply so assigned, precisely because in this he is *one* as God and man.

majesty, lordship, dignity, power, effected by the principle of love (thus a unity quite different from all other indwelling and gifts of grace)—does not lie in the intention of their positive statement. Both in their insistence on full humanity and full deity, and in their approach to the nature of the unity, they remained true to the witness of the New Testament. What requires to be done is to press beyond the suggestion of a merely fortuitous, accidental or conjunctive unity, which might be given by their description of "moral" or "personal" union, to a recognition of the truly ontological or metaphysical character of the unity which is involved in relation, of man to God and of God to man in Jesus Christ.

If what we have said of the constitution of finite selfhood in relation to God is valid, then the being of Christ in relation to God is a unity with God, which is not extraneous to, but constitutive of his being as a self. And if God is himself present in the love of Jesus for man, then from this side also, from the side of God's act, the relation is one which gives and determines a oneness in being.

However, this is not the only way in which the unity of Christ is to be viewed. Finite selfhood is not simply a function of its relations to other selves or to God, nor does the divine condescension in Jesus Christ mean that God has ceased to be God and turned into a finite self. Therefore, what has been said so far about the oneness of the incarnate Lord must be complemented by other ways of speaking about the unity in him of infinite and finite being, ways

19828

which are not somehow "more" ontological nor another ontological union, but another way of describing the same act of incarnation. This will be a way reflecting the fact the self is constituted not only by its relations, but also and inseparably by being a self in those relations (see p. 92, above).

It was this concern which came to expression in the Alexandrine criticism of the Antiochene formulas and in the church's rejection of (what was thought to be) Nestorianism. It was represented in the doctrine that the two natures of Christ are united in one *persona* or *hypostasis*, i.e., in a "hypostatic" union. Difficulty arises, however, from the fact that the meaning of these terms, even in the definition of Chalcedon, the Tome of Leo, and the synodical letters of Cyril, was by no means precise and unambiguous. And it is possible to discern the presence of several levels of interest and intention in the development of the Christological controversies around this point.

(1) At one level, the intent of the insistence on one *hypostasis* was evidently to stress that in the incarnation a *real* unity of God and man is to be found. To say that Jesus Christ is one *persona* is to designate a unity distinguished from (or "more" than) a unity of "dignity or authority," "conjunction," "juxtaposition," or "acquired participation" (to use the language of Cyril's third synodical letter to Nestorius). It is a way of emphasizing that the Incarnate Lord is one concrete being, a single objective reality, "One and the Same Christ, Son, Lord, Only-begotten." This, I

am inclined to think, is the primary and probably original interest of the formulation.[2]

But something else is involved when the dogmatic statement "one *persona*" or "one *hypostasis*" was explained by saying that the one *hypostasis* of the being of Christ is simply the *hypostasis* of the eternal Word of God, and that the manhood of Christ is "anhypostatic" or (with Leontius) "enhypostatic." For here we have further sorts of interests intermingled. (2) There was the proper and necessary concern to protect the primacy of the act of God in the incarnation; the divine leads, the human follows; it was the Word who became flesh, and not manhood which achieved divinity. But (3) the use of these terms also represented an attempt to *explain* the unity of the person of Christ by way of a distinction between "person" and "nature" or *hypostasis* and *physis*, and involved a kind of meta-psychological interpretation of human selfhood (and a conception of deity) which did not differ in principle from that of Apollinarius.[3] That sort of interest was cer-

---

[2] This is certainly the only clear meaning of "one *hypostasis*" in the formula of Chalcedon and the Tome of Leo, and the basic meaning in Cyril's letters referred to by the council. Cf. T. H. Bindley, *The Oecumenical Documents of the Faith*, 4th ed., pp. 99, 122. It is true that in other writings Cyril does on occasion identify the one *hypostasis* as simply the *hypostasis* of the Logos.

[3] The line from Apollinarius through Cyril to Leontius represents a common tradition and way of thinking. In Apollinarius (because to him the human mind was necessarily evil), Christ has a divine instead of a human mind or spirit (*nous*), together with a human soul and body. In the later theory, Christ has a divine rather than a human *hypostasis*, together with a human mind, soul and body. (C. E. Raven, *Apollinarianism*, p. 297, argues that the differences between Apollinarius and "the whole Greek school from Justin to Leontius and John of

tainly not a part of the concern of Chalcedon. Moreover, (4) the history of these terms seems to reveal a far greater preoccupation with the divinity of Christ than with his true and full humanity.

In view of this, we are required to raise serious questions about contemporary efforts to state the doctrine of incarnation in terms of *anhypostasia* and/or *enhypostasia*, and of the assertion that Christ had not a human but a divine *hypostasis*. It is clear at the outset, for example, that the words *persona* and *hypostasis* cannot mean what in usual parlance is meant by "person" or "personality" or "selfhood." (As soon as, in rejecting monothelitism, it is declared that Christ had both a human and a divine will, this is established.) Now, if the term *anhypostasia* means only that there never was any humanity of Jesus existing apart from the being of God in him, then we must cer-

---

Damascus" are "merely verbal and superficial"; and e.g., p. 238, that Epiphanius and Apollinarius "mean exactly the same thing, so far as he means anything at all, . . . *nous* signifies to Apollinarius what he calls *hypostasis*." Cf. *passim*.)

This line of thinking was throughout concerned with an analysis of personal existence which finds a "place" for the Logos within the structure of concrete selfhood. That this was felt to be a way of insuring real unity in the being of Christ was due to shared assumptions regarding the meaning of passibility and impassibility. But, as noted below, the whole weight of the argument that this sort of conception describes a real unity of the being of Christ has to be carried by the theory of the way "nature" is related to "hypostasis" (or, in Apollinarius, of *nous* to soul and body). Whether we call this a "psychological" or a "metaphysical" interpretation is unimportant. It is important that Chalcedon does not reveal concern with this sort of analysis.

The same understanding of passibility and impassibility made it impossible for the Antiochenes to state their conception of the union of God and man in Christ in a way which seemed to mean more than conjunction or juxtaposition.

tainly affirm it. Jesus was not somehow first a man, and then also the eternal Word. Also, if *enhypostasia* means more positively that the human nature of Christ has its concrete and true human existence only in union with the Word, and that precisely in this union is he united personality, then again the concept is of value. It emphasizes that the truly human nature of Jesus' being depends upon the union with God, and that apart from this his humanity would not have been full and real, but a broken and lost manhood.[4]

To say this sort of thing is to reaffirm the first two levels of interest distinguished above. And that is essential. But it may be doubted whether the terms *anhypostasia* and *enhypostasia* do this in an appropriate way, and whether they are not so much involved with the third and fourth kinds of interest as to be quite unacceptable statements about the unity of God and man in Jesus Christ. Thus it is alleged, quite in the traditional language, that the hypostatic union means the presence in Christ of the *hypostasis* of the Logos, which already possessing the divine nature assumes human nature. The human nature is anhypostatic, it has no human *hypostasis*, no finite center of individuation, and is therefore universal or generic manhood which becomes concrete and particular (enhypostatic) through union with the *persona* of the Word.[5]

However, this insistence that the unity of Christ's being

[4] This interpretation of *enhypostasia* is suggested by Prof. Edward Hardy. It would seem to lead us somewhat in the direction of the concept of unity described at the beginning of this section.
[5] Thus, e.g., E. L. Mascall, *Christ, the Christian, and the Church*, p. 19 (cf. chs. I and II). Following Leontius, Mascall holds that *enhypostasia*

is established by the presence in him of only the one *hypostasis* of the Word is both doubtful and puzzling. It is puzzling because of the mechanical, even physical, conception of essential unity which is implied, because (apart from the doctrine of *communicatio idiomatum*) the divine and human are brought together simply at a point (yet not really at that point, for there is only the divine *hypostasis*, therefore the unity is given only by the inherence of human nature in the divine *hypostasis*, and everything turns on the theory of the relation of *hypostasis* and nature), and because of the emptiness of the concept of universal humanity in this connection.[6]

The interpretation is doubtful because the attempt to distinguish between the fullness of human nature and "person" or *hypostasis* requires a truncation of the full manhood of Christ, by omitting the concreteness of being a particular human being, a self, the center of personal relations, i.e., his being *a* man. When, for example, a distinction is drawn between the "person" of Jesus as the divine "subject" or center of experience, and the "human nature"

---

refers to the human nature's being made concrete and particular through union with the Word, but it is clear that this does not mean the particularity and individuality of a *human* personhood. Leontius adopted the term *enhypostasia* to counter the contention of the monophysites that every complete nature must have a *hypostasis*, but it is difficult to see how this is more than a purely verbal or formal change, since the *hypostasis* in which Christ's human nature is made concrete is still no human *hypostasis*.

[6] We may sympathize, of course, with the desire to affirm that in the incarnation, Christ participates in the whole of humanity, that all humanity is "in him," but this does not seem to be the basic motive in this connection, and in any case, this is an inadequate way of making the point. (Cf. ch. V.)

through which that experience comes,[7] then something clearly essential to full human existence is denied. For to be human means inescapably to be a finite subject of experience, and it is certainly as such that Jesus prays to God, suffers and is tempted, loves God, has faith in him, hopes in God, obeys God and is humble before him. But the effort to distinguish between *persona* and human nature in such psychological terms is not worse than the mathematical analogy, in which the *persona* of the Word in relation to human nature in the incarnation is likened to the point which is the terminus of a line, giving concrete being to the line yet not really taking up any space in the line as such.[8] This sort of analogy is not only a little ridiculous when used as an explanation of the realities of personal existence, but certainly offers no adequate explanation of the unity of the being of Christ.[9]

[7] Cf. L. Hodgson, *The Doctrine of the Trinity*, pp. 68f.; and "The Incarnation," in A. E. J. Rawlinson, ed., *Essays on the Trinity and the Incarnation*, pp. 379, 387, 392. At least Hodgson must be credited with trying to give a clear and meaningful account of the distinction between person and nature, which is better than mere reiteration of the terms.

[8] Cf., e.g., R. Garrigou-Lagrange, *Christ the Savior*, pp. 160f.

[9] The statement of M. Schmaus, in *Katholische Dogmatik*, II, pp. 282f., seems to me to provide an unusually clear illustration of the inherent difficulties in the general view we have been describing, the more so because he tries to give a genuinely metaphysical interpretation which does not abandon personal categories. After distinguishing between "nature," as that which makes a being what it is (man to be man, animal to be animal, etc.), thus the root of the psycho-physical powers through which activity is carried out (e.g., hearing, seeing, thinking, willing), and the "person" or the "I" which possesses this nature and acts through these powers and is thus responsible selfhood (*Selbstand*), Schmaus describes the incarnation as follows (p. 283): "Now the incarnation means that a determinate human nature was so united with the Logos and bound into commonality of being [with the Logos] that it no longer

In trying to understand the difficulties into which the concept of *anhypostasia* can lead, especially in its susceptibility to an interpretation which deprives the humanity of Christ of a genuinely human personal center, it is helpful to recall the basic positive (and necessary) motives behind its use. These are the maintaining of the primacy of God's

---

has in itself a human selfhood, but has selfhood only in the selfhood of the divine Person, that it is no longer the possession and tool of a human 'I,' but of the 'I' of the divine Logos. It is no longer a human 'I' which speaks, acts, thinks, wills with the powers of the human nature, but the 'I' of the Son of God." Schmaus frankly admits the difficulty of this view, when in noting his nearness to the Thomist position he allows that this view "has no right answer to the question, how a human nature can possess its own reality (*eigene Wirklichkeit*) without having its own existential being (*Dasein*)" (p. 293). Moreover, he adds, "it is difficult to show that a real unity between the Logos and human nature is possible, without there taking place on the side of the human nature some kind of real alteration penetrating into the structure of being" (p. 294).

The deficiency of this sort of view, as I have tried to suggest, is that it conceives the problem of the unity in the wrong way, and thus ends in the puzzle about how Christ can have no human "person" yet be truly human. It should be remarked that the proper objection to the denial of human "personhood" to Christ comes not from the monophysite thesis that every nature must have a *hypostasis*, but from the character of human existence, and not primarily from a general analysis of human existence as such but explicitly from the picture of Jesus Christ as presented to us by the gospels. In the gospels, the human subjectivity of Jesus is not replaced by the divine, though it may also be true that God is the ultimate subject of his existence. It would be better to say then, if we were to use the traditional language, that the hypostatic union means the union of two hypostases in one hypostasis, a notion which is not self-contradictory if we properly understand the fullness of God's lordship and transcendence (see below), and which is therefore not a mathematical assertion about commensurable entities. Moreover, we can indeed allow that the incarnation means the alteration of humanity, not in the sense of the substitution of a divine for a human hypostasis, but along the lines suggested at the beginning of sect. 4, above.

In *The Mediator* (pp. 318–320, cf. also 270n., 272), Emil Brunner suggests an interpretation of the doctrine of *anhypostasia*, which is stated in

act in incarnation, i.e., that *he* is the subject of this act, and the designating of the unity of God and man in Christ in such a way as to make it clear that he is one being, one Lord and Son. The problem is that these legitimate ends are pursued in a way which seems to compromise the real humanity.

The root of the difficulty, I suggest, lies in an inadequate

---

genuinely personal categories and yet avoids unfortunate division between a metaphysical self (or center of experience) and human "nature." Brunner distinguishes between "historical personality" and "mystery of personality." Historical personality means everything which is "given" in personal existence, the natural endowments, including individuality. The mystery of personality, however, is "not 'given' but self-determined"; it is the development of the possibility into reality "by means of our own personal act, our own decision . . . action as a whole . . . the fundamental original act." "For 'person' means precisely that which we cannot *have*, but must *be*." That is, the mystery of personality is relational, it is the reality of *responsible* being; "our being, as persons, is determined by our attitude toward God." (This seems very close to what we have earlier described as the theological nature of manhood, above, pp. 94ff.)

In these terms, it is meaningful to say that the mystery of our personality is *sin*. Therefore, Brunner asserts, Jesus Christ has human historical personality, but not the human mystery of personality: "although He assumed human nature with its possibilities of being tempted, . . . He did not assume human personality in the sense of the ultimate mystery. Instead of the human mystery of personality, sin, He possesses the divine mystery of personality: divine authority."

The difficulty with this statement is that even here something is omitted. For in contrast to the mystery of personality which is sin, i.e., disobedience and irresponsibility, we ought to think of true human personality as the ultimate act of obedience and responsibility. And surely we must ascribe to Jesus Christ not only the divine authority, but also the mystery of true and responsible human obedience (as we have argued above). Brunner's failure to do this is perhaps related to his tendency elsewhere in *The Mediator* to think in terms of noumenal/ phenomenal distinctions in personality and to his conception of the relation of eternity and time.

conception of the relation of Creator and creature, which is not truly drawn from the incarnation but from other sources. It may appear in crude form, in which the presence of God in Christ is described in ways which obviously deny the reality of the human existence and the form of the servant. Or it may appear in more subtle form, as the assumption that God can be present in Christ, and real unity of being established, only by being present as (i.e., by providing for, and therefore displacing in man) something (however small) which ordinarily characterizes human existence. In either case we have to do with a conception of transcendence, or ontological distinction, which is of a spatial sort and does not really express the radical transcendence of God. It understands the ontological presence of God as somehow necessitating the absence of finite being, and the subjecthood of God in act as excluding the subjective agency of man.[10]

This seems to reduce the relation of Creator/creature to

---

[10] The same problem is reflected in one aspect of the controversy between Athanasius and the Arians. The Arians understood the transcendence of God in such a way as to make him the utterly aloof and absolute Unity who is related to the world only through the Logos, the Logos thus being God only secondarily, relatively and derivatively. Athanasius, however, viewed God primarily as Perfect Being, who does not need an intermediary to be in relation to created beings but is in himself directly in contact with the created order. Here we have to say that it is Athanasius, and not Arius, who really holds to the transcendence of God; for just because God is really transcendent, and not just another finite being, we can say that he throughout relates himself to the world. Thus in respect of the incarnation, because God is truly transcendent and almighty, he is able to be present in Christ without destroying or replacing the humanity or any portion of it.

a relation between two finite entities, and to deny the real freedom and transcendence of God in his relation to the world generally, and specifically in the incarnation, as well as to misunderstand the constitution of finite personal existence in its relation to God. But if we are faithful to the biblical witness to Jesus Christ, then we have to take his person as the final source of our understanding of divine freedom and transcendence. And in the New Testament, this consists not only in the power, glory and majesty which raised Christ from the dead, but the power, glory and majesty of birth and crucifixion. That is, the superiority of the divine being is such that it cannot be defined simply as the opposite of the human (this has been a frequent error in the discussion of human passibility and divine impassibility). God is no prisoner in his elevation and distance. He is the really free and transcendent One, who because he gives man existence in time and space over against himself, is able to enter that existence and make it his own without abolishing the existence of the creature, is able to be the Subject of a human life and work without destroying the human subjectivity of that life and work. It is the lordship of God which is the lordship at the same time of humiliation and exaltation.[11]

[11] The point we have been making has also important relation to the question of the sinlessness of Christ. Here we must say that Christ *could not* sin because he *did not*, and he did not because he *would not*. That is, sinlessness is not a static, impersonal state, but a willed reality. Ability not to sin and inability to sin have to be interpreted in terms of genuinely personal existence, rather than impersonal concepts of passibility and impassibility. (Thus also, sinlessness is not negative, referring to the absence of something, but a positive perfecting and

Now I do not propose that this perspective solves all the problems of the unity of God and man in Jesus Christ. But it does, I think, begin at the right place, with the fullness of humanity and the fullness of deity in the one historical figure. It suggests that our understanding both of man and of God must be laid at the feet of Christ and conformed to the light of his being. Our view of his humanity must be transformed to acknowledge the being of his selfhood in movement to God, seeing the unity from the manward side; and our view of God's being in him must be reinterpreted in the light of the full manifestation of divine glory and freedom, which is God's giving himself in love and condescension, i.e., in the self-movement of his coming to be truly present in Christ, so assuming

---

fulfilling in the midst of real temptation and struggle [see ch. V, sect. 2].) And here the questions of the sinlessness of Christ and the unity of his person come together. In the classical discussions, at least following Athanasius, it was argued that Jesus Christ must be truly God if we are to have any real hope of salvation; salvation cannot be made dependent on an accident or a changeable essence. But changeable and unchangeable were here thought of in quite impersonal terms of mutable and immutable essences. Thus it was that Apollinarius found it necessary to say that in Christ the human *nous* was replaced by the Logos; for if Christ had a free human mind, then our salvation is dependent on a changeable essence. The same pattern of thought was reflected in the conceptions of *anhypostasia* and *enhypostasia*. The difficulty is that when we speak in such terms, it is impossible to speak of real uniting of the immutable and the mutable. But if we are willing to think of genuinely personal existence and will, with reference both to God and man, then we can speak of real uniting, of the informing of the human by the divine fidelity and unchangeableness. The whole human personality of Christ was so conformed to God that he, as man, would not and therefore did not and could not sin. His subjectivity (or selfhood) as man was thus conformed to and the instrument of his subjectivity as the Word.

(or embracing) the reality of the human life of Jesus in his own being present that the life is both wholly his act and the act of the man. So we can speak of God and man united unconfusedly, unchangeably, indivisibly, and inseparably. And if this does not remove the "paradox" and mystery of the one being of Christ, and I do not intend that it should, it at least helps us to specify the paradox in terms conformable to the fullness of the New Testament witness, and it places the mystery of the unity where it belongs, not in the puzzle of how man can be man without a finite center of individuality, but in the mystery of God's being and his freedom to become incarnate for us and our salvation.

ADDITIONAL NOTE A
(see sect. 2, note 6, above)

The quest for the "historical Jesus" has in recent theology become quite unpopular—and perhaps rightly so, as that quest was conceived at the beginning of the present century. Yet I suggest that the criticism of our theological fathers at this point is often both confused and misdirected by failure to distinguish carefully between several quite different problems.

First of all, there is the problem of the limits of historical science, or the nature of historical knowledge. Insofar as the former search for the Jesus of history involved the assumption that the historian can completely disentangle the so-called historical, uninterpreted, human figure from the interpretations of faith, we have to reject it. Neither in New Testament nor any other historical study is the historian able to deal with "bare facts," which are not in some way selected and interpreted. History is remembered history. Since Martin Kaehler's classic critique (*Der sogenannte historische Jesus und der geschichtliche biblische Christus* [2. Auflage, Leipzig, 1896]) and the subsequent work of a generation of biblical scholars, as well as the studies of Dilthey and Collingwood, it is a familiar truth that historical science cannot arrive at a purely uninterpreted "photographic" account of the life of Jesus of Nazareth. (Of course, every photographer knows how silly it is to speak of a photographic record as purely "objective.")

But often intermingled with this problem is a question of a quite different sort. It is most vividly expressed in the assertion that the affirmation of faith cannot be dependent on the results of historical research. Faith cannot be held in suspense until the historian has assured us that after all it is all right to believe. But this is itself an ambiguous sort of statement. It may mean that the confession of faith does not arise simply as the end product of the process of historical study. And that is certainly correct. No amount of information about the historical figure of Jesus can compel the affirmation that he is the Christ. That is the enigma of his personal existence, the mystery of his authority and the being of God in his humanity. And in this sense the confession of faith is independent of the results of historical investigation.

But the same problem is also posed on a different level, in terms of the possible tension between faith and historical criticism. We see this, for example in Brunner's *The Mediator*, when he speaks of the possible conflict between faith and history and concludes that "faith can be combined with all kinds of historical criticism which do not alter the historical image of the existence of Jesus to such an extent that so far as faith is concerned it would be impossible to understand the apostolic testimony to Christ." (*The Mediator*, Eng. tr., p. 168. Cf. the whole of this chapter on "The Christian Faith and Historical Research," also ch. XIV, "The Historical Figure of the God-

Man.") A similar conception of the problem appears in John Knox's *Criticism and Faith*, where the effort is made to show that faith has nothing to fear from the free operation of research, "that biblical historical criticism not only has no stranglehold on Christian faith, but does not have it in its power to destroy one jot or one tittle of the gospel." (P. 21) This is so, Knox argues, because of the essential conjunction of fact and memory and the continuing presence of Christ in the church. Thus he can say that "our knowledge of Christ does not depend upon what can be known about the life of Jesus; . . . our knowledge of the authentic words of Christ does not depend upon what can be established as Jesus' words; and . . . the truth about the meaning of Christ does not depend upon what was present in the self-consciousness of Jesus." (*Ibid.*, p. 47) To be sure, the memory of the church has indissoluble reference to what happened in history, and the event is not to be swallowed up in the life of the community. The occurrence of certain facts is indispensable to the witness of faith, and these are "fully validated by historical study." Moreover, it is possible to distinguish between essential and nonessential elements in the event, essential elements being those "which not only were actually present in it but could not conceivably have been lacking." (*Ibid.*, pp. 82, 89, 86)

The difficulty with such ways of formulating the problem is that they are still restricted to the posing of an epistemological problem. We may well agree that the discernible historical outlines of the figure of Jesus must be such as to make possible the judgment of faith, and that the occurrence of certain events is necessary to faith. But is it not misleading to put the matter this way, as if the problem were chiefly that of reassuring faith insofar as it refers to certain "factual" events?

I suggest that the essential reference of faith in Jesus Christ requires us to ask the question of the historical figure in a different way, and for our purposes a more important way. Instead of beginning with the "how" or "whether," i.e., how the human figure gives rise to the Christological judgment, or whether that figure makes intelligible the apostolic witness, we may start from *within* the confession of faith that Jesus is the Son of God, the incarnate Lord. Then the question becomes "what is it that faith affirms to have occurred?" And we are driven at once to ask as exactly as we can after the historical outlines of Jesus' life. For we do not affirm that the Son of God was incarnate in the memory of the community, or in the confluence of fact and interpretation, but in the person of Jesus of Nazareth. In spite of all its inadequacies, the quest for the historical Jesus had at the center the desire to know all that can possibly be known about the being of the Lord in history. This is something we dare not jettison, and it is an indispensable task of historical research to describe that historical figure, i.e., to assist in grasping concretely the event of incarnation.[1]

In other words, *that* we acknowledge Jesus to be the incarnate Lord cannot be a product of biblical research, but *what* we mean by incarnation can be said only with its aid. I could wish this were not so, for it leaves us with nasty problems. But the conclusion seems to me inevitable as soon as we have said that the Word became flesh and dwelt among us. It is essential to know, for example, what Jesus said, for if his message was simply the proclamation of a coming kingdom of God, the incarnation means one thing, but if he claimed divine authority for himself in teaching and calling disciples, the incarnation means something else. It is also important (unfortunately for our theological composure) to know what Jesus understood himself to be. *Whether* Jesus knew himself to be

---

[1] I think something of this is implicit in Knox's discussion of the creative contributions of biblical scholarship, but it is not worked out. Cf. *Criticism and Faith*, esp. pp. 83ff. and 92ff.

the Son of God is perhaps not decisive for our affirmation that in fact he was. But our understanding of the *manner* of God's being in him will be shaped by our judgment as to whether he did or did not know this. (Similarly, the problem of the "miracles" falls into proper perspective. Their "historicity" is a significant question, not as proof for the truth of the gospel, but in relation to our understanding of the way in which the power and love of God are present in Jesus Christ, i.e., whether the power of condescension and subjection is at the same time manifestly the power of [e.g.] physical transformation.)

The implications of this conclusion lead us into a range of questions with which I cannot possibly deal here, even if I were competent to do so. But the recognition of the problem gives us at least an indispensable guide in the more modest undertaking of suggesting a perspective for a proper doctrine of the incarnation. One thing is quite clear, we cannot talk about incarnation without concrete reference to the historical figure of Jesus Christ—we may even say, to the empirical structure of this personal existence—insofar as the New Testament discloses it to us as the form of God's reconciling presence. This is not to overlook the incompleteness of the records available to us, nor to deny what was said earlier about the impossibility of neatly separating "fact" from "interpretation" in the biblical witness, but only to recognize that the witness itself directs our attention to that which is objective to the witnesses and their witnessing. And in principle here, the much despised question of the "self-consciousness" of Jesus is not different from the question of the whole character of his ministry or the fact of his death. The "self-consciousness" of Jesus may be an historically insoluble question, but that does not make it unimportant.

Chapter IV

THE CHURCH AS BEING AND
COMING-TO-BE

I. THE ANALOGY OF CHRIST AND THE CHURCH

In our attempt to think out together certain crucial dualities which faith apprehends in the being of Jesus Christ and in the existence of the church, it has become quite clear that we have to do with a consistent pattern of divine operation, which is suggestive of a fundamental analogy or congruity between the being of the incarnate Lord and the life of the community which is his church. Why this cannot be more than an analogy, and why this analogy cannot be taken alone, must constitute a central theme of this chapter. But that there is an analogy, and that this is meaningful for an adequate view of the church, will now be evident: the duality (in unity) of the person of Christ, as expressed in the confession that he is truly God and truly man, is reflected in the duality (in unity) of the church as a people constituted by God's act in Christ and living in dependence on God's grace, yet existing as genuinely human community.

More specifically, the coming of Jesus Christ is from beginning to end a reconciling work of God, a work reaching back explicitly to the preparation for his coming in the people of Israel (and perhaps, implicitly at least, to the creation of man for fellowship with God), embracing the whole of his life, teaching, death, resurrection and ascension, and extending to the final consummation of all things. The being of Christ is God's being in him, the eternal Word become flesh, the being of God for man, God himself present to man in Christ, making this humanity his own as the adequate and appropriate organ of his incarnation, both in earthly existence and in the humanity of the risen Lord. Yet this new humanity is unequivocally the life of a man, its perfection is the perfection of human life. It is a humanity defined and constituted in its existence by relation to God, by Jesus' being man for God, but just in this truly man in his sonship, obedience and love, and therefore man among and for men, the first-born of brethren.

Similarly, the church exists as people of God only in relation to God's calling it into being. The movement of its life is unequivocally a response to the movement of God's act, which precedes, sustains and embraces its response. Its being a *congregatio* depends upon its being a *convocatio*. It is given constitutive memory, faith and hope by God's establishment of the covenant with a people he has chosen, by *his* coming in time and space in Jesus Christ, by his promise of fulfillment. Its life is determined by the words, "You did not choose me, but I chose you" (Jn 15:16). Yet precisely in this dependence, the church is defined by its acknowledgment of God's choosing, and thereby as *human* community, a people in social process and in time, and not so only in outward appearance, but in being. It is distinguished from other communities, not because it has a "true" and "perfect" transcendent reality, of which the earthly form is only an imperfect expression, but because the loyalties and signs which are the bonds of its social and temporal existence direct it always to the God who is the source of its being, because its constitutive historical memory is of the event of Jesus Christ, because its common worship is directed to the Lord who calls forth adoration and thankfulness and obedience by his continual presence in grace and love, because its hope is ever in what he has done and will do.

This analogy may be stated in relation to further classical affirmations about the person of Jesus Christ. God and man are present in Christ unconfusedly, unchangeably, indivisibly, and inseparably. This forbids us to assign the life of lowliness simply to the humanity and the glory of transfiguration and resurrection simply to the deity. Rather, just these are inseparable and indivisible. God is present both in the majesty and creative power of the resurrection and in the almightiness of his condescension in humility, suffering and servanthood. Humanity is present both in weakness, socio-temporal limitation and death, and in resurrection and ascension. Further, the new humanity of obedience, lowliness and sacrifice is at the same time the glory of the divine presence and love. And the victory and lordship of God manifest in the resurrection is at the same time the exhibition of the glory of new humanity. That is, the form of subjection to the baptism of water and of blood is the form both of the new exalted humanity and of God's presence, and the form of resurrection is at once the divine victory and the fulfillment of new humanity. The same power which raised Jesus from the dead is the power of suffering and obedience; and both the suffering of the cross and the victory over the grave are the glorious form of the new man. Precisely in crucifixion and resurrection are we directed most clearly to the indivisible presence of God and man in Jesus Christ. Yet without confusion! In the condescension of deity and the exaltation of humanity, God does not cease to be God and man does not become God.

With reference to the being of the church, the words "indivisible" and "inseparable" point first and essentially to the servant-form of the church. As God deigns to assume humanity in the incarnation, he calls the community of his Son into being in the history in which men live. Its existence as human community, enfleshed with the crude realities of man's sociality and temporality, shaped in the particularity, weakness and transiency of human togetherness, is not a human act apart from or in contradiction to the divine act, but the form of God's own act. The human bonds of its unity in time and space are at the same time means by which God binds his people into one.[1] Yet

---

[1] "Inseparable" refers, more specifically, to the union of the church with the risen Lord, but this must be considered later under the rubric of participation and the body of Christ.

without confusion. The servant-form is an exaltation of
the church, a reflection and manifestation of God's glory,
but the church does not cease to be creaturely community.
God's act in assembling the people does not abolish the
reality of human response and responsibility. The being
of the church is inseparable from the rule of God, but is
not to be confused or identified with that rule. The polarity
of God's act and man's response, of *convocatio* and *congregatio*, must be preserved.

Further, it is possible to speak of congruity between the
unity of God and man in Christ and the unity whereby the
church is at once immanent-historical community and people of God. The analogy here relates to that oneness of
Christ's person which we have earlier described as the unity
consisting in and denoted by the movement or relation in
him of God toward man and of man toward God—from
the manward side it is the direction of his being toward
God which makes his humanity what it is, and from the
Godward side it is act of God for man. So also the church
is one in its being both humanly social and for and from
God. Its humanly social reality is formed by the common
direction of its love toward God and man, but it is such
just as God works in its life, as its love for God becomes
a oneness with God in his love for man, and as God gives
himself through it in love. That is, like the humanity of
Christ which cannot be spoken of independently of the
incarnation, the church has no existence as immanent historical community independent of the act of God calling
it and sustaining it in being. More precisely, and positively,

the church lives absolutely in dependence upon the person of Jesus Christ, and not only with reference to his earthly existence but to his risen being in which he continues to be Lord of the church.

Again, as in the incarnation a true and concrete human existence is brought forth which has its true humanness just in its union with God, so in a similar way the church has its dependence on God as real historically immanent center and life. Or, more positively, Christ expresses his lordship over the church in the concrete reality of its temporal being and form.

So far, we can speak of the analogy of Christ and the church as determinative likeness and congruity. The community of which he is Lord reflects in its life the pattern of his being. But this is only an analogy, or better, it *is* an *analogy* and therefore implies difference as well as likeness. The church is not incarnation, and the duality of divinity and humanity in the person of Christ is *not* the same as the polarity of the church's being (it is certainly misleading, and in the strict sense, improper, to speak of the church as "divine"). For Christ is the first-born of brethren, yet he alone is Son "by nature" and he is Head and Lord of the church, present to it and in it as ground of its life. Thus the terms inseparable, unconfused, unchangeable and indivisible cannot mean quite the same thing with reference to the church that they mean in relation to Christ. Moreover, the servant-form of the church is not identical with the new humanity in Christ, and the mystery of the church's holiness is not the same as the sinlessness of Christ. In its obedience and suffering, the church shares in the experience of Christ, but its obedience is imperfect and its suffering ambiguous. The church awaits fulfillment, depending on the Christ who not only was and is, but is to come. The Head is victorious, but the struggle continues fiercely in the body (see below, sect. 2).

This contrast may be put another way by saying that, while the historical figure of Jesus Christ is such as to make intelligible to faith the conviction that he is the Incarnate Word, the historical life of the church is not evidently such as to make intelligible many of the claims made for it. Certainly it is *called* to be the people of God and the body of Christ, and it is affirmed to be a *holy* nation and a *royal* priesthood, but the call seems to have met with distorted response and the theological claim seems quite inconsistent with the facts of its life. In the church we meet rebellious rejection of the "servant-form," and idolatrous desire for the "lord-form." Thus in insisting on the truly historical being of the church as human community, we seem to have deepened the problem. If we are able to illuminate one side of the dialectic (or one of the "paradoxes") of the church's being by seeing it in the light of the incarnation, we at the same time expose the more sharply the other side of the dialectic, its real dissimilarity to the incarnation and the inconsistency of its life.

2. THE CHURCH IN SIN

The crux of the problem is embraced simply by the word "sin." The duality of the church's being as at once humanly historical community and a people wholly dependent on God for its people-hood is paralleled by the duality (or "contradiction") of the church's holiness and sin. And one is tempted to say that the latter is the real problem, that the former question is merely a difficulty for thought, which is settled in principle as soon as we acknowledge that God does in fact work in the world and which is thus essentially of interest only to theologians who like to speculate on the manner of divine operation. But the problem of sin in the church!—that is the real question, and a matter of the liveliest practical as well as theoretical import. Now this is obviously an artificial and misleading distinction, and I think it can be shown that these two problems belong together, for both questions relate to the ontology of the church and to its practical task. But first it must be recognized that the question of holiness and sinfulness in the church is a real, and not merely an apparent, problem.

I stress this because of the attempt frequently made to deny that the church *qua* church is involved in sin: that individual Christians may sin, that indeed every individual Christian is a sinner, but the church as such is holy and free from sin. Now, of course, it is usually said at once that whatever holiness and perfection the church has is entirely a gift from God, that it is the holiness of Christ in the church—and certainly that must be said, with both positive and negative implications thereof. But as soon as this is interpreted to mean that the church, when it is *truly* church, embodies fully the holiness and sinlessness of

Christ, we are driven into one of several unsatisfactory positions. Either this means that a distinction is drawn between the saints, who constitute the true church, and the sinners, who belong externally to churchly institutions—a view which presupposes a thoroughly unbiblical notion of the sanctification of the believer and an intolerable division in the church. Or, it merges with some sort of distinction between an "invisible" or spiritual or inward church, which alone is characterized by the holiness of Christ, and the "visible" or outward or institutional church, which is characterized by sin—a concept which we have found reason to reject as both vague and an implicit denial of the real humanity of the church. Or, it rests on a view of the present transformation of the human community which means that at least in certain aspects of its life (e.g., its dogmatic formulations, its sacraments, its ministerial succession) it is through the work of Christ and the Holy Spirit already made perfect, delivered from the realm of human sin and disobedience, if not also from the sphere of historical contingency and social influence.[1]

A full view of this last conception will appear only as we explore carefully the meaning of the body of Christ and the work of the Holy Spirit, especially in relation to tradition in the church. But a right understanding of these mat-

---

[1] This is, of course, the form in which the assertion appears in some Roman and Anglo-Catholic thought. Cf. the encyclical of Pius XII, *Mystici Corporis Christi* (1943). Also H. de Lubac, *The Splendour of the Church*, pp. 76f. But it is important to recognize that the same basic judgment is made by others of a quite different theological tradition, only in different form.

ters itself requires the acknowledgment that the church in history is *qua* church defaced and marked by sin, and indeed in every aspect of its existence as community of response to the gracious activity of God whereby it is constituted and sustained in being.

In other words, the life of the church cannot be understood simply as analogous to the life of Christ; it reflects also the life of Peter, and even of Judas. The being of the church is congruous with the existence of the believer as justified sinner. More strongly put, the being of the church is not something apart from the fellowship of sinners; it *is* the community of sinful men in which Christ exercises his Lordship. The dialectic of the holiness and sinfulness of the church derives directly from the dialectic of the life of the Christian man as saint and sinner. (This, of course, does not mean that the church is itself a sinning agent, for the church is not as such a personal agent at all.) The attempt to abstract the church from the ambiguity of the life of its members, by affirming that the sin of the members does not touch its true and incorruptible being, implies either the effective removal of the church from the scene of human history (therefore the reification of an abstraction) or it makes nonsense of any talk about personal existence in community. *If the church is called to be a community of Christ in and among men, and indeed true human community, then its being is indissoluble from the being of its members.*

The life of the Christian, as portrayed in the New Testament, cannot be described in a few words (and certainly the phrase *simil justus et peccator* is only a useful symbol for a central feature of that life). But at the risk of gross oversimplification, we can point to certain aspects of Christian existence which are illuminating for the problem before us. The Christian life is described as a life "in Christ," i.e., as a participation in his life, death, and resurrection.[2] It is a constitution of his new humanity in us, both as the norm of our humanity and as the forming of our selves according to the pattern of his person. It is our adoption as sons, who through participation in his sacrifice are forgiven and restored to the status of a child in the Father's house. It is a sharing in that unity of Christ with the Father which is expressed in the constitution of his humanity as man for God and man for man. Here we have to speak of real transformation and new humanity, not in the sense of a new (*noumenal*) self which replaces the old or is hidden behind the visible self, but as the newness of a self which is set in a new relation or context of God's grace and which expresses that newness in the concrete form of living, supremely in love for God and neighbor. We are to take nothing away from the often startling changes in ordinary living which result from men's coming to be in Christ. The New Testament is clear witness that being in Christ involves the manifestation of the fruits of the Spirit.[3]

[2] Once again we must defer further development of this theme to our discussion of participation.

[3] There is no problem here of imputation versus impartation. Both are to be affirmed (and both are stoutly affirmed in Luther's tremendous stress on justification). The real question is the meaning and nature of impartation; only in these terms can the issue properly be drawn.

But precisely in this it is also clear that we are yet in sin. Transformation is not transfiguration. In Christ, one sees himself for the first time truly as sinner, and the life of the saint is marked by the fullest recognition of sinfulness. We have only the first-fruits of our redemption, and we live in continual need of forgiveness. Therefore the Christian life is always a state of hope, of looking to a final consummation, a coming into the fullness of inheritance.[4] That is, the life of the Christian is an eschatological life, a life directed not only backward to what has been done but just because of this forward to what is to be. It is life essentially of movement, of going to meet God in Christ. It is an active waiting for the fullness of participation in the resurrection of Christ. This is summed up in the figure of the Spirit as the *earnest* of our redemption, which assures us that we are in fact set in relation to a fullness that is to come but at the same time that this fullness is *to come*

---

[4] Cf. esp. Rom 8:23–25: "we ourselves, who have the first fruits of the Spirit, groan inwardly as we wait for adoption as sons, the redemption of our bodies. For in this hope we were saved. Now hope that is seen is not hope. For who hopes for what he sees? But if we hope for what we do not see, we wait for it with patience"; Eph 1:18: "having the eyes of your hearts enlightened, that you may know what is the hope to which he has called you, what are the riches of his glorious inheritance in the saints . . ."; Eph 1:13f.: "sealed with the promised Holy Spirit, which is the guarantee of our inheritance until we acquire possession of it"; Heb 6:5: "have tasted the goodness of the word of God and the powers of the age to come."

In these and similar passages, it is clear that the awaited fullness is not just a glorification of already perfected children, who are rewarded for present trial and tribulation, but a completion of their (very imperfectly begun) growing up to the stature of the fullness of Christ and the final establishment of victory in the struggle of the Spirit against the old humanity.

(II Cor 1:22; 5:5; Eph 1:14). Thus the new humanity is formed and constituted not only by what it has been and is now made but by what it is to be.

Just here we are able to see the relevance of this description to the being of the church. It is not that the individual is prior to the church, or that the church is a collection of individuals, but rather that the church does not have its being apart from the intertexture of the lives of its members and therefore it shares fully in the ambiguity of their lives. To speak of the possibility of sinfulness of all the members of the church, yet without the church being involved in sin, is simply nonsense in view of the existence of the church as real community. It is not only that individuals fail, but churches fail. Nowhere is this more clearly seen than in the Apocalypse, where it is churches as such which are accused and called to repentance and renewal.[5] Have they ceased to be churches? No! Just in their sin, their faithlessness, disobedience and betrayal, they are still churches. Similarly, the community to which Paul writes in Corinth is a community wracked by sin and division, yet he describes it as church in the most extravagant language. And in I Peter (4:17) it is declared that judgment begins with the household of God.

The New Testament is filled with criticism and exhorta-

---

[5] Rev 2, 3. The form of address in these chapters is of course to the "angels" of the seven churches, but it is clear that in this the Spirit is speaking precisely to the *churches*. Cf. the repeated demand, "He who has an ear, let him hear what the Spirit says to the churches" (2:7, 11, 17, 29; 3:6, 13, 22). The address to the "angel" of each church serves, in part, to emphasize the corporate character of each of the communities.

tion, and nowhere in this, I think, do we have warrant for drawing a distinction between the sin and holiness of the individual and the sin and holiness of the church. While the exhortation is addressed in form (and often quite specifically) to members of the church, to say that their sin refers only to their individuality and not to them as members of the community [6] is to be quite false to the New Testament understanding of the corporate existence of persons in community. Indeed, the full horror of the sin of the Christian can be seen only as it is recognized that he sins as one who has been made a member of Christ and therefore involves the whole church in his sin.

It is quite unnecessary to remind ourselves at this point of all the sins of the church in history. The imperfection is all too obvious. What is important is to recognize that as the church has its being in truly human sociality, in which it expresses the pattern of God's condescension in the incarnation, it exists in that sociality as a community in sin which requires to receive cleansing from its Lord. And this means that its reality, like that of the individual, must be defined also in terms of expectation. (This way of speaking in itself suggests a too sharp distinction between the community and its members. It is useful for the purpose of analysis, but the community and its members are not related as "also" or merely "like," for the community is not apart from its members and the members not apart from the community.) The church has its being as historical com-

---

[6] It must also be said, of course, that it is of the essence of sin to try to deny the being of the self in community.

munity of faith and love in dependence on God, not only in relation to what God has done in Christ and to the present lordship of Christ and work of the Spirit, but in the awaiting of its fulfillment. Its being is a being of movement and direction, of going to meet God in Christ, of hoping in the promise.

Moreover, the End toward which the church looks has reference not merely to the church, but to the whole world. It is the End in which *every* knee shall bow and *every* tongue confess that Jesus Christ is Lord, to the glory of God the Father (Phil 2:10). And if in a certain sense the church stands over against the world in respect of this end, it at the same time moves toward the end together with and in the world (cf. ch. VI).

3. THE BRIDE OF CHRIST

This understanding of the being of the church comes to expression clearly in the image of the Bride of Christ, as adumbrated explicitly in Ephesians 5 and Revelation 21 and 22. Certainly this image denotes the intimacy and permanence of the union of Christ and the church (Eph 5:25, 31f.), and like the image of the body, it portrays the necessary subjection of the church to Christ, its head and savior (Eph 5:23f.). But it is at the same time an eschatological image. "Christ loved the church and gave himself up for her, that he might sanctify her, having cleansed her by the washing of water with the word, that the church might be presented before him in splendor, without spot or wrinkle or any such thing, that she might be holy and without blemish" (Eph 5:25–27). This language may suggest to us not only the completed act of the passion, a consecration and cleansing already wrought for the church, but also a presentation and union in perfection which is to come. That is the more clear as we see this passage in the context of other New Testament figures and statements which cluster around it. Thus St. Paul speaks of betrothing the Corinthians to Christ, as the church to be presented to Christ as the pure bride (II Cor 11:2). And in the Apocalypse the image of the bride is decisively an eschatological figure. Here the church can by no means simply be identified with the bride of the Lamb who has made herself ready for the marriage (Rev 19:7; 21:2). The perfect adornment (21:2, 10ff.) and readiness of the bride belong to the time of the consummation which is yet to come. Meanwhile the church exists in the time of struggle and decision, for over against the figure of the bride is the figure of the harlot (ch. 17ff.), the enemy yet temptation of the church. The church is faced with the supreme choice between love and lust. The church is chosen to be the bride of Christ, thus chosen to choose Christ, and now exists in the tension of choosing between Christ and Satan (who has also chosen the church and is hardest at work in it). Judgment and transformation stand between the church and the marriage supper of the Lamb (ch. 21). Moreover, there is no simple identification of the church, even as purified, with the bride, the holy city, the New Jerusalem. A new heaven and a new earth are brought into being (21:1). *All things* are made new (21:5). What is involved is a transformation in which the distinction between church and world is done away with. There is "no temple in the city, for its temple is the Lord God the Almighty and the Lamb" (21:22).[1] If then the church is the bride, it is the community which is yet coming to meet Christ in final fulfillment, a fulfillment which involves the entirety of the new heaven and the new earth.

Again, the imagery of the Apocalypse brings together the figure of the bride with the figure of the wedding feast, which also refers to the union of God with his people and which appears repeatedly in the gospels as an eschatological symbol. And the image of the wedding feast can perhaps in turn be related to the Last Supper and the Eucharist, as the celebration in the church which directs attention to Christ's coming again in the great feast of the Last Day.[2]

Thus the image of the bride may lead us to the heart of

[1] If we take this with proper seriousness, the present being of the church is "relativized" or qualified not only with respect to its own need of cleansing and perfecting, but also as a being (i.e., in distinction from the world) limited to the time before the End. That is, the consummation of the church is its dissolution, precisely by the inclusion of all things in union with Christ—yet this is really the fulfillment of the church (see ch. VI, sect. 4). This has important implications for the notion of the "church triumphant."

[2] The Old Testament image of the marriage of Yahweh and Israel also bears an eschatological note, but of a different sort. There the marriage is already sealed in the covenant, and marked continually by apostasy, i.e., adultery, on the part of Israel. Thus the required fulfillment and purification refers to the marriage which has already taken place. In the NT, however, the marriage is not yet completed, the church remains the betrothed. Yet the tension in the life of Israel is not left behind in the new covenant; apostasy occurs here also, and the cleansing and uniting with Christ by its very nature involves expectation of final completion and perfection.

the mystery of the church's being. If it speaks of the union of the church with Christ, it also defines the nature of that present union by referring to a union which is to be. The church is subjected to Christ as its savior, and remains until the last times the betrothed being presented to Christ.[3] The

---

[3] Cf., e.g., H. de Lubac, *The Splendour of the Church*, p. 51, where this is allowed, though only in a limited (I should say, too limited) sense: "Prior to the Incarnation, before she had become the Bride, she was the Betrothed only; and that remains true to a certain extent right up until the end of time, in that the mystical marriage of Nazareth and Calvary still needs the last Parousia as a complementary: 'That is the wedding of the Lamb, when the Church shall be united with the Lord in the bridal chamber of the heavenly kingdom.'"

De Lubac does not seem to allow the full force of his citation (from St. Bede the Venerable), which clearly denotes the full eschatological character of the image; the *wedding* is the final union of the Last Day. De Lubac does speak of the continual liberation and purification of the church from her spiritual prostitution (cf. p. 73), but even for him the dominant note of the image of the Bride becomes always the union already established, the already received betrothal gift of the blood of Christ (p. 51), so that the relation between the present and future states is fundamentally one only of development and completion rather than of continual, final and thorough restoration (cf. pp. 41f.). The communication of grace to the church is such that in certain crucial respects renewal is not necessary, for the church is already impeccable and indefectable.

Yet it must be recognized how far de Lubac goes in the right direction, in contrast to those who would make the historical form of the church (in particular the hierarchical principle) extend into eternity, who "are unwilling to admit that on the day of her triumph the Church will abandon 'her mortal and historical clothing'—that is, 'all that aspect of herself by virtue of which she is actually . . . the instrument of her own growth and a partaker in the earthly condition of her members.'" (p. 46; cf. pp. 46ff.)

It may be suggested that much of the fanciful and extravagant development of the idea of the Bride comes from a failure to recognize the importance of its eschatological reference. Cf., e.g., E. L. Mascall, *Christ, the Christian, and the Church*, pp. 124ff., following the lines of Claude Chavasse's *The Bride of Christ*; here the marriage is simply something which has already occurred.

cleansing of the church is an act completed *in Christ* for the church, in his giving himself up for the church in order to consecrate her and cleanse her. It is a completion in the church inasmuch as Christ embodies the church in himself. But just as Christ is the Lord who was and is and is to come, so the church needs continually to be cleansed of her sin, in which she yet lives, and awaits her presentation to Christ in splendor, holy and without blemish.

The implications of this understanding of the church, as existing not only in flesh but in sinful flesh, and therefore determined in an essential manner by the expectation of the fulfillment, lead us in several directions. First of all, they remind us that the analogy to Christ can only be an analogy. The historicity and sociality of the church reflect the humanity of Christ. As his earthly life was a recapitulation, a perfecting of manhood through the whole course of life, so the life of the church is a continual growing up to the stature of adoptive sonship. The church is called to the way of humility, of becoming last for the sake of the last and the lost, thus to the glory of Christ's way to the cross. But this way in the church and this growing up are at no point wholly free from sin, from groaning and yearning for fulfillment, from the struggle between the flesh and the Spirit. The consummation will not be the manifestation and glorification of a perfection already achieved in the church, but radical cleansing and transformation. Therefore the forms of the church's existence in history are without exception under God's judgment. Its participation in the forms of human community and temporality reveals at once the gracious form of God's working, and a sharing in the human body of sin. The order of the church is ambiguous, and in the Lord's Supper the community is ever reminded of the promise of necessary renewal and re-creation. The life of the cross in the church is both a suffering for humanity and a judgment upon the sinfulness of the church's flesh.

Only in this light are we able to speak properly of the transformation which is now present in the life of the church. In the scriptures, the sacraments, the confessions, the ministry and ordering of the church, the mission to unbelief, the fellowship within the community, the service in love to the need of man and society—in all this God has taken unto himself the minutiae of human existence, to use them for the accomplishment of his ends and thereby to transform them, to constitute them as forms of genuine human response to himself. But because that response is yet sinful response awaiting the day of its consummation, none of the forms of response can be taken as in itself pure and undefiled (and thereby irreformable). The Word of God is given in scripture in the stumbling words of men and is heard only in constant struggle to interpret its meaning, in the dimness and perversion of our understanding. The thought-forms of an age which make it possible to present the gospel meaningfully in creed and confession are the same forms which can blind and distort the vision of men and which must ever anew be crucified with Christ that through them he may be present to men. In the sacraments, and supremely in the Eucharist, the church confesses weakness and the need to be purified and fed by the presence of Christ, in forms which are explicitly related to the life of the church as the impure servant and which look to the day of consummation when these forms will pass away (and the justification of the sacraments is found partly in the fact that they point not to themselves but to the Christ who was and is to come). The ministry of the church is confused with the ministry of men and must ever be subjected to Christ's own ministry. The fellowship of the church becomes a mere expression of group togetherness. Spiritual and moral pride infect the church with special virulence, and the witness of the church continually has to be redeemed from being self-defensive witness to itself. In every respect, the forms of the church's life continue to be subject to the judgment of God, in order that the form of the church may be reformed and conformed to God's own humbling.

Of course, the eschatological character of the church's existence is not simply a function of its sin. It derives directly from the church's establishment in Jesus Christ, which points immediately to that which is to come. The Lord's call, to repent for the kingdom is at hand, is also on the lips of the church. The powers of the New Age, which are already at work, direct the attention of men to what is yet to be. The reconciliation which has been accomplished in Christ refers also to the final redemption in which the mystery will be made manifest and all things brought by Christ to the Father. The recollection of the coming of

Christ in incarnation is inseparable from the expectation of his coming again.

This can be put in language suggested by Karl Barth's discussion of the *time* of the church, as the time between the *parousia* of the forty days and the final *parousia*, i.e., the time graciously given by God who does not speak his final word without waiting upon the response of men in faith and praise, thus the special time of the mission of the church, of the response and responsibility of man to the work of God, the time of the church for God and for the world.[4] It is the time beginning with the Ascension, in which Christ is present to his people in a different way. He is not less Lord of the church, in this time between, but his lordship is acknowledged also and indispensably in the awaiting of his coming in fulfillment. As he was once visibly present as Lord of the church, so at the End he will again be visibly united with his people. The growth of the church is meanwhile never complete and perfected, not only because of creatureliness and sin, but because of the boundary set by God's determination of the church as a temporary and partial representation of that new humanity which will be established fully and finally only in the coming kingdom. The church's union with Christ must be viewed in relation to the final time, to an end and goal toward which not only the church but the world moves. The existence of the church is thus, from the nature of its origin, calling and sustenance, a teleological existence.

[4] Cf. *Kirchliche Dogmatik*, IV/1, pp. 810ff.; also IV/2, pp. 709ff.

4. ESCHATOLOGY AND THE ONTOLOGY OF THE CHURCH

In sum, the church as the New Community, as the true Israel, as being in Christ, is an eschatological community, a people defined not only by recollection but by expectation, having "tasted the goodness of the word of God and the powers of the age to come" (Heb 6:5) and called to a hope (Eph 1:18) of possession of the inheritance (Eph 1:13). Though we now live in the world as a community whose Lord is Christ, yet "our commonwealth is in heaven, and from it we await a Savior, the Lord Jesus Christ, who will change our lowly body to be like his glorious body, by the power which enables him even to subject all things to himself" (Phil 3.20f.). The church lives at the point of overlapping of the two ages, the old and the new, the present age and the age to come. Its time is a time of warfare between the powers of this age and the power of the age to come, and not as if the church were simply the representative and embodiment of the power of Christ and the Spirit over against a world (i.e., non-church) of evil and darkness, but rather as the church shares in the struggle in its own life and therefore awaits the fulfillment of God's purpose for itself.

If this is taken with the seriousness which the New Testament seems to require of us, then the problem arises how we are to understand the eschatology of the church in relation to its ontology, the being of the church in relation to its coming-to-be. Are we to absorb ontology into eschatology, saying that the being of the church is not in what it *is*, but is found simply in what it is *to be?* [1] Or, shall we say only that the church is both ontological and also eschatological, both a being and a becoming?

It seems to me that both these questions involve a false statement of the issue, implying that the two dimensions, if not incompatible, are at least of such different orders that they cannot really be brought together, but can only exist in tension with each other. I would suggest, on the contrary, that they must be brought together and thought into each other. It must be affirmed that statements about the eschatology of the church are themselves judgments about the ontology of the church. What the church is to be is a determination of what it is; the future of the church defines its present.

The necessity of the attempt to think these dimensions into each other springs from the resistance of the New Testament to any effort neatly to divide present and future states of being. The present age and the age to come do not lie in a simple succession on a chronological time scale; the two ages are present together. [2] The End is "breaking into" the present. Thus the New Testament can also speak of

[1] This seems to me a tendency in the otherwise excellent statement of L. Newbigin, *The Household of God*, pp. 149ff. The conclusions which Newbigin draws here seem to me in the main correct and essential, but his argument requires a more adequate relating of ontology and eschatology than is made explicit.

[2] On the other hand, the eschatology of the NT cannot be made into a simply vertical eschatology, with the coming of the kingdom being only the immediate relation of each moment to a transcendent realm. The kingdom is not only "looked up to," it is "looked forward to." The reference to the future cannot be excluded.

the church's already being what it will become. Christians must consider themselves really dead to sin and alive to God (Rom 6:11). The church *is* the body of Christ, is cleansed and holy, is in reality and not only in ideality one, whole, and without blemish.

The problem is to try to say this meaningfully, without appeal to some esoteric gnosis. We may try to do so by analogy with various aspects of the church's being (or ontology) already delineated. First of all, the church is constituted by what is done for it in Jesus Christ. In him fulfillment is achieved, the re-creation of humanity accomplished, the perfection of cleansing and union with God already wrought out in the life of man, the resurrection a fact in history. The church exists in absolute dependence on this act. Whatever justification and reconciliation, or cleansing or unity or newness of life, is present in the church, is received from Christ. He alone is in himself whole and without blemish, and the church has these qualities only as it depends upon and shares in him. But this is not an act done simply "upon" or "for" the church. It is the creation of the church as human community in its concrete historical remembering of Christ, a relation in which he is genuinely present to and in the church, and in which its life is defined and determined by his presence. Its being is constituted by its past, which is not something the church has left behind, but which enters into its present. More specifically, the church is what it is because its self-identity as historical community rests in what God has called it to be in Jesus Christ, because its humanity is formed around his New Humanity.

But this past is present. The calling of the community into existence is not an isolated act of God relating only to a particular moment in time. As Christ is risen, so the act of God in constituting the community is an act which embraces the whole of its life, and its being a society is determined by the direction of its love and worship in the now toward the God who meets it in the living Christ and works in it as Holy Spirit. Or, to put it the other way around, the commonality of loyalty and adoration, which makes it really a community, is grounded in and determined by the Object of that relation. Thus the being of the church as a genuinely human historical community is defined by the movement of that communal life in response to the movement of God in its living past and its present, and thereby (since it has its being in that relation) as a participation in the perfected humanity of its Lord and as the existence of a New Community. Therefore, it will not do to ignore or minimize the reality of transformation in the church, the extent to which God has in fact made the vessel of its humanity a presence of his grace, the manifest obedience to Christ (and this not least in the church's humbling of itself in the confession of sin).

In these ways of speaking about the church, we are helped in seeing how it has its being not purely "in itself," nor even in an *esse* delivered over to it from God, but always as being-in-relation to God in Christ through the Spirit. Precisely in its existence as a socio-temporal human society, it exists by an openness to God. Thus, to say that the church lives by the mercy of God is not pious sentiment, but a statement about the ontology of the church, which defines its self-existence as inseparable from and determined by its existence in dependence on God.[3]

The same pattern of thought needs to be applied to the church in relation to its future, its coming-to-be. From the "human" side, this is to say that the community exists as much by virtue of its hope as by reference to its memory or its present faith. These are quite inseparable elements. The expectation of the church is determined by its recollection and its recollection is incomplete without its expectation, and both are present in its love for God (thus the expectation of the church always takes the form of the coming again of Christ). The community can understand what it now is only in the light of what it will be, for it *is* only as it is *becoming*.[4] We might say that the nature of the church can be specified only as we take into account its "final cause," though remembering that that term can here be given meaning only with reference to what God will make of the church.

Thus the constitutive hope of the church is a hope in God. Hope, as the human side of the church's direction toward the End, must be seen in the context of God's de-

[3] Cf. what was said in ch. III concerning the nature of humanity (esp. sect. 3). Cf. also ch. VII for a fuller discussion of the "role" of the Spirit in this relational existence.

[4] This is not to reduce being to becoming, but to say that being is dynamic, it is at once being-in-becoming, and specifically in reference to personal and communal existence.

termination of that End. The church in expectation, as in recollection and in worship, is formed in response to what God has done, does now, and will do, which are held together in the unity of God's time. By God's act, the past, present and future of the church are brought together, not in the abolition of temporality or the freedom of the future, but as in himself he binds past and future together and is compresent to men, as he meets us in the past which lives in the present and meets us in the future which rushes into the present. The Christ who is to come is the same as he who has come, thus to be "in" him who was means to have our being in his awaited coming. In this sense, the future is determinative of the present, making it what it is. And the being of the church is a being-made in movement toward final consummation. The future really remains future. The church is yet to become what it is to be, and "it does not yet appear what we shall be" (I Jn 3:2). We know only "that when he appears we shall be like him, for we shall see him as he is" (*ibid.*). Yet just because the church is set in relation to the end and goal of God's final word, because this *is* its future, it is determinative of the nature of its present. The church is what it is because it is turned toward the End which God will accomplish. The community exists in active relation to that future, which is a coming-to-be, and not merely what some day will be.

In this way, the peculiar complexity of the church as a people living at once in the present age, with all its ambiguity and evil, and in the age to come, appears perhaps in clearer light. The church is given the earnest of its redemption, it does manifest the first fruits of the Spirit, the new humanity of Christ is at work in it—and in this sense it is proper to speak of its growing up into Christ, of development, of completion in final union with Christ. But just as in this the church is dependent on the divine mercy, so it receives in relation to that which is to come. The Spirit is the Spirit of hope, the gift of the Spirit an earnest of an inheritance yet to be possessed. The holiness and unity of the church are throughout the holiness and unity of Jesus Christ, the incarnate One, the risen and living Lord, the bridegroom whom it goes to meet—for it has its being, is constituted, is what it is, only in relation to him. It claims nothing for itself, but only for Christ whom it recalls and expects. It therefore lives in contrast between what the life of the church now is and what it is called and intended to be, thus in repentance—yet repentance in relation to what is really coming-to-be, and therefore in justification. The holiness and unity of the church are as filthy rags, but because it hopes in Christ it is purified as he is pure (I Jn 3:3). The wholeness and cleansing which it does not yet possess are nevertheless present in its life, already grasped by its hope. In the church there is forgiveness and reconciliation, the life of new humanity, because the *congregatio* of repentant sinners is a response to the divine *convocatio*, because the faulty and divided memory of the community is united in the oneness and perfection of the

One who is remembered, because the hesitant love and questionable obedience of this people are directed to the real Lordship of Christ, and because even in the faintness of its hope it is bound to and shaped by what is really coming-to-be.

Chapter V

THE BODY OF CHRIST

I. THE IMAGE AND ITS CONTEXT

The image of the "body of Christ" is without doubt one of the most tantalizing of all the figures which in the New Testament are applied to the church. As the object of very lively reappraisal in recent theology, both Protestant and Catholic,[1] as the figure which is in some ways the most fully developed of New Testament designations for the church, and as a concept accepted in some form in nearly every variety of Christian thinking, this image obviously provides an indispensable category for theology of the church. Yet it would be a grave error to take this image in isolation from other figures, or to assume that this is the one concept to which all others must be subordinated and in terms of which they must be interpreted.[2] That is why it is possible to deal directly with the figure of the body only at this relatively late point in our discussion.

---

[1] Cf. the very useful summary of the recent revival of the concept of "mystical Body" in Roman Catholic thought, in H. de Lubac, *The Splendour of the Church*, pp. 6off.; also the extensive historical survey of E. Mersch, *The Whole Christ*.

[2] See Additional Note B, at the end of this chapter.

Any interpretation of the assertion that the church is the body of Christ must set this phrase in the context of all the other ways in which the New Testament speaks of the church.

"Church" and "body," we must remember, are explicitly connected in only five of the New Testament writings, and all of these from the "Pauline" corpus—Romans, I and II Corinthians, Ephesians and Colossians—whereas other images appear both more widely and more frequently in the New Testament. This is not said to decry the importance of the figure of the body, but it ought to put us on guard against exclusive preoccupation with this image. That is the more necessary because the image of the body is constantly interwoven with other designations and figures (cf. esp. Eph 2:13–22 and 5:21–32). The New Testament writers use many expressions which are complementary, cognate or even synonymous, and move back and forth from one to another without hesitation. Moreover, the figure of the body is itself employed in different ways and with varying associations of meaning, which may change even within the same passage. Sometimes the stress is on the harmonious relation of the members of the body (e.g., I Cor 12:14ff.; cf. Eph 4:11f.), sometimes on the subjection of the body to the head (Eph 5:23) or the life which comes to the body through the head (Col 2:10, 19), sometimes on reconciliation into the unity of the body (Eph 2:13–22; 3:6; 4:4). It is essential therefore to see the various functions of this image in relation both to each other and to different ways of speaking of the church, and to try to hold all of these together.

One important clue to the significance of the body-figure, and its prominence in the Pauline literature, is its relation to the problem of the unity of the church. Nearly all the explicit references to the church as the body of Christ are directly connected with this problem, either in the discussion of the image itself or in the context.[3] Here we see reflected Paul's almost constant preoccupation with division and disunity in the church, a preoccupation necessitated by the realities which he faced. Not only in respect of the parties at Corinth or the conflict with the Judaizers, but also in relation to a host of petty jealousies and disputes, Paul was fighting for the unity of the church. And it was a real fight, as John Knox has shown in his book, *The Early Church and the Coming Great Church.*[4] This is a most significant fact, and if we remember that Paul was writing to concrete situations, and not merely expounding transcendent wisdom about the "nature" of the church with-

[3] The passages which explicitly connect the figure of the body with the unity of the church, are I Cor. 6:15; 10:16f.; 11:29 (if "body" here refers to the church, as seems likely); 12:12–27; Eph 2:13–22; 3:6; 4:4; 4:11–16; Col 2:9–19; 3:15. The problem of unity is of course manifold; it may mean outright division and dissension in the church, or it may mean (as in I Cor 6:15; 10:16f.; 11:29) the betrayal of life in Christ which is a breach of community. Rom 12:4f. is a reflection of the problem as expressed in I Cor 12:12ff.

It is significant that all but one of the other "body" passages also refer to the relations within the body, and specifically to the headship of Christ (Eph 1:22; 5:23, 29; Col 1:18). They are thus not foreign to the problem of unity. Only Col 1:24 stands alone here.

[4] Cf. *op. cit.,* esp. ch. I and pp. 88f.

out reference to the needs and problems of these to whom he wrote, we are helped to understand why the image of the church as the body of Christ played such a large role in his thought. This is not necessarily to say that the concept of the body appeared simply in response to the problem of unity in the church, nor to limit its significance to that, but it does illuminate a dominant and pervasive feature of the form and employment of the image—namely, the stress on the true and inescapable sociality of the church as membership in Christ and in one another.

This understanding of the image is reinforced by the fact that it consistently deals with life within the community, more than with the relation of the church to the world. In the uses of the figure of the body, as Ernest Best points out, "the relationship of the Church to the world outside is never discussed. . . . The metaphor looks inward and not outward; it is used, not to express a truth about the place of the church in the world, but about the relationships of members of the Church to Christ and to one another; it is concerned not with the external life of the Church but with its internal life." [5] If that is so, then it is at once clear that the image of the body needs not only supplementation by others but complementation—but more important, we are directed to the real center of the various configurations of ideas, both of the body image and of the other figures, viz., the person and work of Christ and the Spirit. The "body" is *of Christ*, in him we are one body and members of one another (cf. Rom 12:5), and Paul speaks

[5] *One Body In Christ*, pp. 188, 113.

of unity "in Christ" even before he writes of oneness in the body (cf. Gal 3:28).

Behind the metaphor of the body stands the conception of *participation* in Christ, or life in and with Christ, and on this the notion of the body essentially depends, for our relation to one another in the church derives from our relation to Christ. The figure of the body appears to be a further development of the understanding of unity with Christ, and distinctively as this bears on the relations of the members. The reality to which the image of the body refers is in the first instance membership or life in Christ, described both as being "in Christ" and "with Christ." [6] It is difficult to exaggerate the importance of this idea for Paul. It appears constantly and in all his letters. Paul affirms that Christians are already "in" Christ, not just striving to be in him, but now acting and living in Christ and he in them.[7] They are related to one another and "are one" in him.[8] God acts toward men "in" Christ, he forgives, gives grace and eternal life, redeems and saves, gives himself "in" Christ [9]—and these affirmations have the double reference to the being of God in the historical figure of Jesus Christ and to the accomplishment of his redemptive activity through the believer's participation in the historical person. Both individuals and groups are said to be "in Christ," [10] and being in

[6] Cf. Best, *op. cit.*, pp. 1ff., 44ff., for an exhaustive study of the occurrences of these terms.

[7] E.g., Rom 8:1; 9:1; 16:3, 9, 12; I Cor 3:1; Col 1:28; Gal 2:20; Phil 1:26, 3:1, 3; 4:4, 10; Rom 15:17; I Cor 1:31; 15:31; II Cor 10:17; Col 2:6.

[8] E.g., Rom 16:2; I Cor 4:15b; Phil 4:2; II Thess 3:12; Gal 3:28; Rom 12:5.

[9] E.g., Eph 4:32; 1:16; Col 1:14; I Cor 1:4; 15:22; Gal 3:27.

[10] E.g., II Cor 5:17; 12:2; Phil 1:14; 3:9; Col 1:2.

him are never as isolated individuals but always with others in a whole. The term "in Christ" is closely connected with the expression "with Christ," particularly in the theme of dying and rising with Christ. The believer has already died with Christ, has been baptized into his death, yet Paul can also speak of a present dying (or suffering) with Christ.[11] The Christian is now risen with Christ—i.e., he has been made alive in Christ, Christ is his present life—yet he hopes for and awaits the fulfillment of his rising with Christ (specific references to the resurrection of the Christian, as distinct from the possession of new life, usually refer to the future).[12] While the phraseology "with Christ" may be contrasted with the term "in Christ" in that it lacks the explicit note of relation to others, so prominent in the use of "in Christ," both expressions convey the idea of participation in Christ. It is not just a dying and rising "like" Christ, but a sharing in his own death and resurrection. The basic thought in both terms is union with Christ himself.[13]

2. INCORPORATION—PARTICIPATION

1) In short, in order to deal with the conception of the church as the body of Christ, we must first speak about the meaning of participation or incorporation in Christ—and this in turn must be approached in the first instance and

---

[11] E.g., Rom 6:3–11; Col 2:12–3:5; I Cor 15:31; II Cor 4:10–12; Phil 3:10.

[12] E.g., Rom 6:4, 5, 8; 8:17; II Cor 14:14; Eph 2:4, 5; Phil 3:21; Col 2:12, 13; 3:1, 4; I Thess 4:14–17.

[13] Best suggests, op. cit., pp. 60, 62, that a sequence is evident here. We die "with" Christ, and then are "in" him. "With Christ" describes the source of the Christian life; "in Christ" refers to the subsequent nature of that life. But this distinction is not important for our present purposes.

fundamentally from the side of God's act in Christ. The principal word is a word about what God has done, not about that state of the believer. It is the word of incarnation and atonement, and specifically of the full participation of Jesus Christ in humanity and his incorporation of humanity into himself. This is a theme which we have already explored in part, in describing the humanity of Jesus essentially in terms of his being man for man and man for God, i.e., a true humanity which is constituted as such in the fullness and perfection of relation to others and to God (see ch. III, sect. 3). What now needs to be added is that just this way of being truly and perfectly man is a taking up, a drawing, an incorporation of humanity in himself.

This affirmation is to be made in several ways, or on several levels. First, it refers to the assumption in the incarnation of human flesh and blood, mind and spirit, i.e., of the concreteness and finitude of human embodiment, sociopsychological structure, historical particularity and experience of God. In itself, this is a being united to the whole of humanity, an identification with the race, a sharing in the oneness of the children of Adam. This is as it were the ground floor of the participation of the incarnate Son in the whole of mankind, and of mankind in him. But beyond this is the very definite and explicit way in which Jesus Christ binds himself to men, and them to him, in a humanity from first to last given for and to others, in deeds and words of love, forgiveness and healing, in taking their needs to himself, in pouring out body and soul even unto death for them and their salvation. He makes himself one with them, and draws them to him, by the fullness of his self-giving, which is constitutive of *his* being as man. As *this* man, whose personal existence is what it is only in this complete interrelationship with others, he becomes one with all men.

But more than this! Jesus Christ comes into the midst of, and makes his own, the situation of sinful humanity. The humanity which he takes is not a humanity miraculously preserved from the struggle against the "body of flesh." It is a humanity in which that fight is carried on in all its intensity, and with victory. The humanity assumed by the Son of God is not the innocence of the fresh-created humanity of Adam, now appearing in the middle of mankind's sin, but it is the same humanity of the children of Adam—i.e., "fallen" humanity. The humanity which Jesus Christ takes and heals is precisely that which man has become in estrangement from God. Temptation to despair and disobedience is as real in him as in any man; indeed, we may say that only he knows the true depth of temptation. Yet without sin! That is the sinlessness of Jesus, that he who was made to be sin knew no sin, that in this humanity, this sinful social texture, sin is overcome. He becomes what we are, but he does not do what we do. To put it another way, this is the miracle of incarnation, of the unity of God and man in him: the perfection of his humanity is not something separable from the dwelling of God in him; it is wrought out in the oneness of God and man in his person; and apart from this unity, his manhood would not be that of whole and perfected humanity, but that simply of lost mankind.

This is the center of the problem of unity with Christ. It is not merely a question of separation in time and space between ourselves and Jesus Christ. That is a real question, and cannot be avoided. But the distance is not only spatio-temporal; it is the *distance* of sin which must be overcome.[1] Incarnation and atonement are here absolutely inseparable. We have to do not only with the coming of God into humanity, but with a coming in reconciliation. Only through reconciliation can unity with Christ be described. And the crux of his being one with us lies in his identification with our fallen state. In his baptism in the Jordan he affirms his solidarity with sinners, and this is the pattern of his ministry. The center of his uniting himself with the whole of humanity is the cross, as the Judge accepts judgment as his own, taking on himself the condemnation which belongs to mankind. Here the distance is overcome. The perfection of his humanity is no longer the great obstacle to being one with him, but the very possibility of being "in" him; for that perfection is wrought out of our lost situation, and precisely as Christ makes that situation his own. The distance is overcome just in its being established.

On this basis, it is possible to speak of the victory of Christ not simply as the victory of an individual, but of the people in him. To be sure, it is for him a fully personal and individual struggle, and thus he is our brother and ex-

[1] Cf. K. Barth, *KD*, IV/1, pp. 315ff.

ample. But the depth and intensity of the struggle is even greater, for he stands before God and against evil as the Messiah, who will not be alone in this, who represents and embodies in himself the people, whose anxiety is not alone for himself but for the people, whose decision and victory are for those with whom he has made himself one. This is supremely to be seen in the temptation and the passion. The victory over temptation in the wilderness is the conquest of the attempt to lead the Messiah away from his identification with sinners—by saving his own life instead of fasting, by establishing a kingdom on the pattern and under the aegis of the lordship of evil (instead of the lordship of suffering and identification), by trusting God in the wrong way (again by claiming special exemption for himself). So also in the garden, the final temptation is to prevent the triumph of evil over his own person, in disobedience to the will of God and again by breaking off the way of identification with sinners.[2] Thus in all this the struggle of the whole people is involved. The decision is for them and extends to them, and because of it Christ is not only brother and example but source and head of the community. The same thing is to be said of his positive obedience of suffering in the passion. The suffering is because of identification with sinners and for their sake. It is an assumption of their suffering. The offering up of his life is not simply the freely trusting and obedient returning to the Father of an individual life which has been received from him, but a sacrifice and self-giving for those

[2] Cf. the long note on the temptations in Barth, *KD*, IV/1, pp. 286–300.

whom Christ lived to seek and to save. Precisely at the point where he seems to be most alone and deserted by men, he makes himself most one with them and takes to himself *all* (whether fearful disciple, or fellow crucified, or crucifier).

Here we must bring together the themes of representation, substitution and incorporation. Representation and substitution become merely artificial categories of a legalistic atonement theory apart from the acknowledgment that the one who is representative and substitute is genuinely one with mankind, i.e., has his being as person in binding himself indissolubly to men and lifting them up in himself. But incorporation cannot be spoken of apart from representation and substitution; these are essential modes of incorporation (thus it is false to oppose "covenant theology" to "theology of the body"). This is especially clear in the light of the constitution of humanity by relation to God. Jesus Christ takes mankind into himself by standing in its place of judgment and sacrifice; he substitutes himself for us, takes our place, and thereby makes himself one with us. He represents us, stands for us, acts on our behalf, intercedes for us, so that his being truly man for God is a being on our behalf, a headship of a new humanity, an act and decision which not only influences but already reaches out to include our act and decision. Thus Christ is both *a* man before God and *the* man before God; his is the humanity of one who will not be and is not apart from the rest.

Finally, the act of the incarnate Lord in taking man to himself must be viewed in the light of his risen humanity and of the consummation of all things. His identification with men does not cease with the crucifixion and resurrection. The incarnation has a beginning but no ending. The Christ who rises from the dead does not shed his humanity but lives (the resurrection of the body), and is so present to men, with his people even to the close of the age. He makes intercession for them, and through the Spirit he continues to give himself to men, working in them the pattern of his humanity, the mind which is his mind. He continues to bind men into himself, into the fullness of his humanity, not by dissolving their humanity into his but in the nearness of his individuality which forms and shapes their manhood. Yet that working is not yet complete, the presence not face to face. Christ's identification with man in the days of his flesh and the presence of his risen humanity in the church point forward to the final uniting of all things in himself, to the new heaven and the new earth, to the final speaking of God's word, to the fullness of cleansing and the uniting of mankind in the perfection of Christ's humanity (see ch. IV, sect. 3). Christ's incorporation of humanity into himself is not alone something to be looked back upon, or presently realized in the church, but is also awaited.

2) We have so far been looking at incorporation or participation in Christ from the side of God's act in Christ. This must also be interpreted in terms of the response of the community, which remembers Christ, believes in Christ, hopes in Christ, and whose members are said to be "in" him.

Christ's taking of our humanity into himself is the ground and possibility of that movement of our selves, whereby through the Holy Spirit the work of Christ in humanity becomes not only for us and upon us but in us. His openness to us and binding himself to us call forth an openness and binding on our part. Here we have to speak of faith as the expression and means of participation in Christ.

Faith here means the total response of the self to the act of God in Christ—believing, trusting, accepting, obeying, loving, hoping. It is the decisive movement of the self in relation to the ground and source of its being, thus no mere "moral" quality or "psychological" state, but an ontological act penetrating to the root of selfhood. Nor is faith a "supernatural" addendum to a "natural" whole. There is no "natural" self which stands outside the relation of faith or sin (see ch. III, sect. 3). Faith and sin refer precisely to the self in unity and wholeness in relation to God. Thus we cannot contrast a "supernatural" with a "physical" or "dynamic" or "historical" efficacy of God's act.[3] The grace which comes to us in Jesus Christ is not some "thing" issued by and thus apart from God, but God's being himself present to us, re-creating the structure of the relation between ourselves and himself. Grace *is* the new structure in which we exist. So also faith is the indispensable reorientation and

[3] Precisely here we must reject the customary Roman conception of grace in favor of a more biblical ontology of grace (and of selfhood). And, as suggested in Additional Note B, at the end of this chapter, it is that false understanding of grace which results in the usual Roman concept of the "supernatural" and "mystical" body of the church.

restructuring of our selves, through which his gracious act is made effective in the reconstitution of our existence.[4]

It is helpful to describe this movement from the side of the believer as a relation or condition of openness of the self to Christ, a determination of the self with reference to his being the chief person in the community. This is a manifold openness. It means that Christ becomes part of our past, indeed the determinative moment of our past. He is remembered not as an item in an indifferent reporting of an ancient world foreign to our personal world, but as the central figure in a story which has been made our story, and therefore by a remembering which makes him genuinely present in our life. This past lives in us and we in it. To take Christ as our past means to be drawn into the event of his life, so that the great decision of our life is the decision already made in Christ, the pattern and strength and goal of our life is the life already lived out in Christ in growing up into the fullness of perfect humanity, the victory already accomplished in him. The past which is in us is a new past, a history characterized by the law of the spirit of Christ instead of the law of sin and death.

But this openness to Christ refers not only to his being present to us in that remembering which joins our life story and his. It is also an openness to his present risen Lordship. He comes to us not only through the mediation of historical memory and the outworking of his new hu-

---

[4] This means also that Christ is received in the eucharist *in faith*. He truly presents himself in the sacrament, but our participation in his presence is effective only through faith.

manity in the intertexture of the community which he formed, but in his immediate presence as the risen and ascended one, freed from the physical limitations of space and time. Response to his present lordship means accepting, and thereby being joined to, his obedience to the Father. It is sharing in his everlasting love to man, and joining in his sacrifice and intercession. Through the Spirit, i.e., by the working of the Spirit *in* us as the ground of our response, we are joined to the Christ who now lives and rules and are formed in his image. The pattern of his life is made the pattern of our life in communion with him, the love of God is poured into our hearts. Thus we share in his life in a way decisive for the being of our selves. As we said earlier (ch. III) that human nature is what it is, is constituted, in relation to God, and true humanity in dependence on God in faith and love, now it needs to be said, more specifically, that the new humanity of the Christian man is formed and constituted as a joining with, a sharing in, and dependence upon the God-manhood of the risen Christ.

Again, the openness to and receiving of Christ is expressed in *expecting* Christ and hoping in him. This is the openness of the life of confession of sin and need, of the acknowledgment that the fullness of life which is in our past as the event of Christ is not yet fully appropriated by us, that we are yet growing up to the stature of the manhood of Christ, that we share only most imperfectly in his obedience and love, that the warfare between the powers of the new and the old ages continues in us. Therefore our life is marked by longing for completion and purification in the Last Day. This is not to be taken as a denial of our sharing in Christ, but precisely as an expression of it. Especially in confession and hope is the life of the believer genuinely turned toward Christ and open to him, thus centrally determined by his presence and joined to him.

The complex pattern of relationship we have been describing can also be stated in terms of various aspects of the life (or body) of Jesus Christ.[5] The new birth of the Christian in the Spirit, which is in part to be described as the entering into a new history and identification with the story of Christ, is an entering into the birth of Christ, the beginning of the new and perfected humanity. The testimony of the Christian to Christ in spoken word and praise, the acceptance of the norms and ends of the kingdom proclaimed by Jesus, and the reflection of his love and obedience in deed, is an entrance into the word and work of Jesus Christ. Conformity to Christ in the acceptance of suffering which comes from the yielding up of self in obedience to God's ordering of life, in self-denial, in sharing the suffering of the world, and finally in the acceptance of death, is an entering into the crucified body of Christ— the marks of which we bear (cf. Gal 6:17). Similarly, the concrete experience of new life in the Spirit, of victory over evil, of the first fruits, of inward and outward transformation of our selves, is an entering into the risen and

---

[5] Cf. G. W. Bromiley, "The Spirit of Christ," in *Essays in Christology for Karl Barth* (ed. T. H. L. Parker), pp. 149f.; also in the same volume, R. S. Wallace on "The Christian Life," pp. 257ff.

glorified manhood of Jesus Christ, into whose image of glory we are being transformed, though we wait upon the day when we shall share finally in his risen life.

Now to speak of these dimensions of the response of faith to God in Jesus Christ is to say that the Christian man shares or participates in the being of the incarnate Lord, that Christian life is life "in" Christ. Participation, we may say, means having one's being fundamentally in another— though without, of course, loss of selfhood or absorption into another. And in the ways we have been describing, we are able to see how the life of the Christian in relation to Jesus Christ means participation in *his* humanity. The relation to him designated as faith, obedience, acceptance, love, hope, etc., is not an "external" relation, an "accident" in contrast to "substantial" selfhood, but a relation which enters into the fabric of personal existence in such a way as to determine its nature as personal existence. As the being of the self is constituted indissolubly in relation to other selves and to God, the new humanity in the church is formed and constituted by being drawn into the event of the life of Jesus Christ.

Participation in Christ may be described after the analogy of our participation in one another in the complex interrelation of life in community, both in space (i.e., in relation to other contemporary selves) and in time (i.e., in relation to past selves). It may be designated as sharing, with Christ and with others, in covenant responsibility. It may be spoken of in terms of action, as the pattern of the life of Christ is embodied in the life of his followers. It may be referred to under the rubric of hope, of life lived toward and determined by its completion and perfection in union with Christ in the kingdom. And in all these ways, the humanity of the Christian man depends upon and is drawn into the being of Christ, so that he confesses "I have been crucified with Christ; it is no longer I who live, but Christ who lives in me; and the life I now live in the flesh I live by faith in the Son of God, who loved me and gave himself for me" (Gal 2:20).[6]

This understanding of participation may be summed up as a sharing in Christ's sonship to God, as adoptive sons. That is, it is his taking us into his humanity as a being of man for man and for God, thus into that oneness with God which is constituted by his believing, obeying, loving, and hoping in God. This is an "adoptive" sonship, because it derives from his incorporation of our humanity into himself and our life in him through faith. It is really sonship, however, because this means not merely a likeness between the humanity of the Christian and the humanity of Christ but a real sharing (albeit incomplete and imperfect) by the new humanity in the church in the crucified and risen manhood of Christ.

3. THE UNITY OF THE BODY

In the light of this discussion of participation, we are able to see the importance of the image of the church as the

[6] The second half of this verse must not be omitted, for it guards explicitly against any sort of absorption or replacement of the believing self. And if the argument of the preceding pages is sound, we need not interpret this saying simply as paradox.

body of Christ. The reality which the image designates is first and fundamentally the participation of the believer and the community in the life of Christ. But that idea leads inevitably to the relation of believers to one another in Christ. Participation is never in isolation but always in community. One is never alone in Christ. Membership in him is at the same time membership in one another. There is no purely private Christianity, for to be in Christ is to be in the church, and to be in the church is to be in Christ, and any attempt to separate relation to Christ in faith from membership in the church is a perversion of the New Testament understanding.[1] The conception of the body, then, is a corollary, or another facet of the union of the believer with Jesus Christ. And while the idea of unity with one another is implicit, and at times explicit, in the idea of participation in Christ, it is in the image of the church as the body that the whole area of relationships of the members comes most vividly to expression.

Central in the idea of the body, as already noted, is the emphasis on the *unity* of the people of God, the oneness of the body. But the nature of the unity suggested by the figure of the body presents yet serious problems. For ex-

---

[1] Schleiermacher, in *The Christian Faith*, §24, gives classic expression to the misleading dictum that in Protestantism the individual's relation to the church is dependent on his relation to Christ, while in Catholicism the individual's relation to Christ is dependent on his relation to the church. It is interesting that while this distinction has subsequently enjoyed great vogue, Schleiermacher himself does not really adhere to it in his systematic discussion, and in effect abandons it in favor of a much more biblical view of the relation of Christ, the Christian and the church.

ample, Paul's employment of the image recalls in part the Old Testament concept of racial solidarity,[2] whereby the sin and deliverance, judgment and blessing, of one, involve the whole people, past, present and future. Israel is constantly viewed as a unit: as a vine or a vineyard, as a sheep, a horse, an inheritance.[3] More important, the nation is the wife of Yahweh (Hos 1–2; Jer 3:8; Ezek 16; etc.), or the servant of Yahweh (explicitly in Isa 41:8ff., probably also in the "Servant" songs). Israel is personified in Jacob and bears his name; and the figures of Adam, Abraham, Moses and Elijah are both individual figures and embodiments of the race.

But if such conceptions as these lie in the background of the image of the body of Christ, and help to explain Paul's use of the phrase, they also seem to emphasize the distance between Hebrew and modern thought-forms. And the Pauline concept may go even further than the notions of personification or racial solidarity. He speaks of becoming one body with a prostitute, and sets this in opposition to membership in the body of Christ (I Cor 6:15f.). More important, Christ for Paul is not simply the embodiment of the people or its dominant member, but the source and life of the community, which depends upon him. And in *Ephesians*, the "one new man" (2:15) which is the church,

[2] This is not to contend that Paul's doctrine roots exclusively in the OT conceptions. Other possibilities have been suggested (see, e.g., the useful summaries in E. Best, op. cit., pp. 83ff., and J. R. Nelson, *The Realm of Redemption*, pp. 67ff.), but certainly this is one important (and perhaps the most important) source for Paul's concept of solidarity in the body.
[3] Cf. e.g. Ps 80:8ff.; Hos 10:1f.; Ezek 19:10–14; Isa 4:1ff.; Jer 12:10; 50:17; Isa 63:13; Ps 33:12.

is created *in* Christ, and the "body" is explicitly that of his person.

Yet neither in the concept of participation in Christ nor in the idea of the body is the fullness of individual personality lost! The church is a plurality of persons in responsible individuality, who as such labor, stand fast, rejoice, have duties and responsibilities. Though Christ lives "in" the believer, it is the believer who trusts, obeys, hopes and loves. If he is never alone in relation to Christ, but in the body, yet it is he who is so related to Christ and the other members. The many are not swallowed up in the one, but remain many members (cf. Rom 12:4f., and numerous similar passages). A corollary of this is found in the "separation" or distance which is established between Christ and the church. It is impossible to say simply that the church, as his body, is identical with Christ. Especially in the earlier epistles is Christ pictured as over against the church; he is its Savior and Lord. But even in Eph 5:21–32, where in terms of the body the unity of Christ and the church is most strongly emphasized, the church is subjected to Christ as its head, stands over against him as the bride who is loved (yet as his own body), and is saved and cleansed by him.[4]

---

[4] Thus Karl Barth is very careful to distinguish between saying "Jesus Christ is the community" and saying "the community is Jesus Christ," or "the Kingdom is the church" and "the church is the Kingdom." We can say that Jesus Christ is the church (i.e., he is the reality of the church), but never that the church is Jesus Christ. Cf. *KD*, IV/2, pp. 741ff. While we may question whether Barth's way of putting this is not unnecessarily paradoxical, certainly the order which he insists on, and the distinction which it implies, is correct.

This fact ought to make us wary of interpreting the figure of the body in terms of "organism" or "corporate personality." [5] These concepts have the value of making clear, that the unity of the community is *in Christ*. But, quite apart from the fact that these categories are not readily available for our thinking about community, if indeed they are available at all, they often do not give the full value to personal individuality which seems to be represented in the New Testament.[6] It is not enough, indeed it is a distortion, to say simply that the believer or the church is "included" in the personality of Christ. Even if we restrict our attention to the image of the body, without reference to all the other ways in which the New Testament speaks of the

---

[5] Best argues, op. cit. *passim,* for the notion of "corporate" or "inclusive" personality as the most adequate interpretation of Paul's teaching about the body. Yet this term is admittedly inadequate and a mystery. It is inadequate because it "implies more than is required. It suggests that believers as a body express the personality of Christ. That conception is not present in our formula. It is true that each member of the corporate personality should express the personality of Christ—'Have this mind in you, which was also in Christ Jesus' (Phil 2:5)—but this is not said of the community of believers as a whole. The whole does not act as a whole and represent Christ." (*ibid.,* pp. 22f., cf. p. 57) The term, moreover, does not clearly indicate the unique place of Christ in the community, nor its dependence on him as head and savior.

At the end of his discussion, pp. 197ff., Best seems to start in the direction of some further interpretation of the meaning of "corporate personality," but apart from the brief reference to "fellowship" nothing further is really said. At the end we are left simply with the term.

[6] This is, of course, not always the case. Lionel Thornton, for example, in interpreting the concept of "organism," is very careful to include the really social, to maintain the notes both of identity and of cooperation. Cf., e.g., *Christ and the Church,* pp. 18, 24. Throughout the trilogy of *The Form of the Servant,* as well as in *The Incarnate Lord* and *The Common Life in the Body of Christ,* Thornton develops this balance in remarkably subtle fashion.

church, a dialectic of unity with and distinction from
Christ and others is to be seen throughout. And as soon as
we bring into view other images, the recognition of the
community as a uniting of individuals, of a plurality of
persons, becomes all the more clear. Both sides must be
emphasized, that the faithful man is such as a member of
Christ, and that the body of Christ is an assembly of faithful men.

1) In seeking a positive understanding of the unity or
solidarity of the community, denoted by the term "body,"
it is useful to begin with recognition of the concrete ways
in which individual selves are bound up, or united, with
the lives of other selves. As we have already seen, the texture of social relations in which human personality exists
(and alone can exist) enters into the very constitution of
personal existence. We are never ourselves simply in ourselves, but in relation to others past and present. We have
our being in the communities of which we are a part, and
are thus "solid" with other members of the communities,
"participating" in them (albeit in quite various ways and
highly fluctuating degree). Now this intense sociality of
personal existence is in itself not adequate to express what
we need to say about the unity of the community as the
body of Christ, but it must be included. It is essential to an
understanding of the church as the realm of grace or redemption, for here we are able to see clearly a way in
which we are never alone in sin or salvation, but always
in our responsibility set in the midst of a social situation
which involves us at every point in sin and grace. We are

not redeemed in isolation from society, but in and with it. Or, to put it another way, the process of redemption includes the shaping of personal existence from the beginning in the historically immanent life of the Christian community. Certainly in this sense, we must speak of social solidarity or unity with one another. This is a body of righteousness and peace in contrast to the body of sin and estrangement, a body of life in opposition to the body of death, i.e., an inter-involvement in social reality whereby we are genuinely members of one another.

2) A further step in defining the solidarity of the Christian community is taken with the recognition that the church is a realm of reconciliation, both between God and man and between man and man. As such, it is the *true* community. This is summed up in I Peter 2:9–10, in the assertion that those who were formerly "no people" have now for the first time become a *people*, viz., "God's people . . . a chosen race, a royal priesthood, a holy nation" —and that precisely through the receiving of mercy, i.e., through the breaking down of pride and egoism which separate men from each other and from God. There is at work in the church a Spirit which creates *new* community, building up by joining men together in Christ (Eph 2:21). By virtue of forgiveness and reconciliation, this community is *the* people, in terms of which all community is to be understood.[7] The unity of the body is a unity of recon-

---

[7] This, of course, not in a static sense of a state simply achieved. The creation of the new community is a continual remaking, as well as a continuation and extension. Further, to say that the church is true community is not to suppose that the goal for the church is to absorb all

ciliation of the two histories and societies, Jew and Gentile (cf. Eph 2:12, 19). And conversely, sin is division and estrangement, the violation of the newly created unity with one another. Sin against the body is that action which disregards and destroys the community of love and reconciliation (cf. I Cor 11:17-29 and 12:4-30). At the heart of sin, as F. D. Maurice constantly insisted, is the attempt to live apart, to be isolated, to cut oneself off from others as well as from God. To violate the body of righteousness and peace in Jesus Christ is indeed to be united with another body, the body of Sin, but this is a less real body, characterized by disunity, by inner separation and estrangement.

The indispensable corollary of this understanding of true community is the acknowledgment that the fullness of individuality is realized precisely in self-giving to others. To exist in the most intimate relation, in union, with other selves is not to be less but more truly individual. The pattern of union in the church is the pattern of the humanity of Jesus Christ, who was the most complete and perfect individuality just in his being most completely and perfectly related to God and man.

3) The unity of the members, as denoted by the figure of the body, may thus be understood partly in terms of our fundamental involvement in one another as selves in rela-

---

forms of community into church community, nor to make the patterns of church order normative for all social order. Rather, in the church is a representation (and very faltering presentation) of the healing, reconciliation and love which God wills to be established in all social forms.

tion, and partly in the light of the reconciliation which defines this community as a people for the first time truly united. But the second of these perspectives leads us further, to a recognition of the ultimate unity of the body. The lateral or horizontal unity, which we have been describing, cannot stand alone, but is based upon and expresses unity *in Christ*. Again, the theme of participation is central. Paul exhorts his readers to be one with another just because they participate in Christ, who is one. The relation of the members to each other is determined by their relation to Christ; the members are one body because the head is one (cf. Eph 4:15f.; Rom 12:4f.; Eph 2:20f.; Col 2:19). That is, the church is said to be the body of Christ because the members are brought together in him.

The unity of the church as the body is thus finally and fundamentally a unity which the community has, not "in itself," but in its head and savior. It is the unity of the one God who has called the community together; it is the unity given to the response in faith by its being a response to the one act of God in Jesus Christ; it is the unity created by participation in his one humanity; it is unity of the one Spirit who works in the church. In other words, it is a unity established and existing in relation to the object of faith and love, the source of forgiveness and new life. Thus, Paul says, to participate in the cup of demons is to be joined in the body of worship and sacrifice to demons, to be partners with demons (I Cor 10:20f.; cf. I Cor 6:15f.). That is no real community, for it has many "gods" and "lords," which are no gods (I Cor 8:4ff.; 10:19); but the worship of these gods means real sharing in the false and divisive body of sin and death. Thus also the "one new man" replaces the "two men," Jew and Gentile (Eph 2:11–15),[8] who were two and divided by hostility because their former unities were not yet the unity given by the cross of Jesus Christ and access through him in one Spirit to the Father.

In other words, the ultimate unity of the church lies in the common object of its memory, faith and hope. It is not ultimately in the apprehending or believing, but in the one who is acknowledged—though unity in belief ought to follow from the oneness of the object. That is, the historical unity of the church is given by the sharing of the whole church in response to the one God, hence in common responsibility to God in Jesus Christ.

That the unity of the church is found in Christ is the ground of both hope and confession in the church. It is the source of hope and confidence because it enables us to say that in spite of tension and division, the church is one. It has an unbreakable unity in the one object of its worship and loyalty, in participation in the one humanity of Jesus Christ. When we look at the "unity" of the church only

[8] While it may be possible to understand Paul's reference to Israel as "one man" in terms of "racial solidarity," this does not help to explain how the Gentiles can also be called "one man" (Eph 3:15). That the latter are "one man" is, however, intelligible when we think of unity given in relation to God, a unity defined by their being "separated from Christ, alienated from the commonwealth of Israel, and strangers to the covenants of promise, having no hope and without God in the world" (Eph 3:12). Similarly, the unity of Israel was really given by the law (circumcision); and the unity of the "new man" is given in relation to God through the reconciliation in Christ (Eph 3:16–21).

in terms of mutual membership in one another or of the removal of distinctions of Jew and Greek, slave and free, male and female—then the divisions of competing national and denominational bodies, of race and class, and of the denial of fellowship between so-called "communions" and between individuals, require us indeed to ask whether in any meaningful sense the term "one church" can be pronounced. Everywhere is given the impression of diversity and plurality, ambiguity and confusion. But even in the midst of that evident disunity and chaos, it is possible to affirm that these divided groups and persons each participate (certainly most imperfectly!) in the new humanity of Christ, are being transformed by him, have community in him, and *in this being bound to him* are one.

Yet just for that reason the church must confess the *sin* of division. The problem of disunity in the church is nothing other than the problem of sin in the church. It is imperfect and incomplete participation in Christ, the refusal of his incorporation of ourselves into his being. It is the distortion and misdirection of faith and hope; and the poverty and impurity of the relation of members to the head are reflected in the disunity and disharmony of the members. In this sense the problem of unity between "churches" is like the problem of unity between persons. And we have to say that at no point has perfection been achieved. The fullness of the new humanity is given in Christ, and participated in by the church, but only at the Last Day will that participation be complete and unblemished, when all things will be subjected to Christ. Meantime, *all* are infected by the sin of disunity and guilty of sin against the body; all stand under the necessity of pressing on toward the goal of mature manhood, of the unity of the faith and the knowledge of the Son of God, of the stature of the fullness of Christ, of the harmonious working of the members of the body. The unity of the church is always in process, a coming to be, a building up of the body, a growing up into him who is the head.

By this fact the problem of the unity of the church is both eased and intensified. It is eased because we are able to say that even now we participate in the unity of Jesus Christ. It is intensified because we can never say finally or exactly how far that unity in Christ is manifested in our visible relations with one another. The line between creative diversity and corrosive division in the church cannot be drawn with precision by us (see also ch. VII, sect. 2). But no one is thereby given excuse for complacency, for we do know that the fullness of reconciliation and unity of Christ are yet awaited, till the Last Day, that we are sinfully divided, and that we are all bound to submit ourselves continually anew to Christ as the head in order that the unity he gives may be expressed in our membership of one another.

4. THE HEAD AND THE BODY

Other facets of the image of the body may be summed up in the dialectic of unity and distinction between the head and the body.[1] 1) First, that Christ is the head means

---

[1] It is especially in the dialectic of unity and distinction that we see the essential difference between the image of the body and the image of the vine. Much that we are saying in relation to the body concept could

that the church is absolutely dependent on him and subject to him. The church exists only in dependence on Christ as the source and object of that memory, faith and hope which shapes the reality of the community and makes it to be. Through the act of God in Christ come the cleansing and reconciliation whereby the company of sinners are made to be one people. There can be no thought of autonomy in the existence of the church, but only of an existence in relation to, by participation in, Christ the head. Therefore the church attributes everything to him, is content to belong to him, to live below him and to follow after him, to confess that all wisdom, holiness, power and glory are his. The church acknowledges that he alone is good and righteousness, and that the holiness and righteousness of the church consist in the confession of guilt before God, by those who know better than others how they continually become guilty before him and one another. The church is sustained by his mercy.

That the church is subject to Christ as the head means also that the church is governed by him through the Spirit, that all decisions, acts and words in the church are subordi-

---

also be expressed in terms of the vine: the unity of the whole, the dependence of the branches on the stalk, the participation of the branches in the life of the stem, and the expression of that life in the fruit of the vine (cf. Jn 15:1ff.). But the metaphor of the vine lacks the note of the "distance," the "over-againstness" or contrast, between Christ and the church which is maintained in the use of the body image, and for that reason the former needs even more the correction and complementation of other images. This difference between the two is also due in part, of course, to the more personal character of body image, which can therefore more easily express the unity in sociality.

nate to his decision, act and word, that he is ever free to dispose as he will of the ways and forms of the church, that infallibility and impeccability can never be claimed for them, that the church must continually listen for his voice and distinguish it from the voices of other lords. This means also that the church participates in him and his work after the pattern of his obedience and servanthood, i.e., by serving him in obedience and self-denial, and that in no sense by taking his place but by allowing him to express himself in the church. As conformed to this pattern of Christ, the forms of church life (which as such are like other social forms) can be and are transformed by the working of Christ in them, becoming forms of service and love.

2) The headship of Christ is also expressed by participation in his new humanity. In response to the confession of sin and submission to Christ, new life is received by the body. Participation of the members in Christ and in one another involves real transformation in the Spirit. Because the great crisis already lies behind in the victory of Christ, there can be a conforming to his humanity and an unfolding in the church of what is complete in him. From him and in him the body is nourished, knit together, and makes bodily growth (Col 2:19; Eph 4:16). As from Adam there is a real communication of sin, not in mere formal attribution nor through biological inheritance, but through the common involvement of men in the social texture in which their humanity is formed, so from the perfected humanity of Christ there is the communication of new life and grace

in the membership of Christians one with another and in the community they have in relation to God (Rom 5:12–21). As the Reconciler and Mediator, the Word made flesh, the risen Lord who is yet with his people, Jesus Christ is the source of life in the community in a far more fundamental way than Adam is the source of sin. It is Christ, not Adam, who is the true head of the race. Through the life-giving Spirit he works new humanity conformable to his own true humanity.[2] This does involve a continua-

---

[2] It is wrong to speak of this new humanity as a "divine" humanity, a partaking in the divine nature (II Peter 1:4) in the sense of a new order of human existence, "higher" than that of the first creation, thus a further stage and level of creation. (Cf. L. Thornton, *The Incarnate Lord,* for an impressive statement of the view that Christ is the beginning of a humanity which stands at a new and higher stage in the evolutionary process. It is a new creation whose relation to prior human nature is comparable to the relation of human to animal creation.) Against this, if we take the witness of the NT as whole, we have to say that the true humanity which is Christ's own and which is expressed in the new life of the community, is *reconciled* humanity, which is not known except as we see it in Christ, but which is our common humanity as it was in the beginning created to be, a humanity truly for God and for man. The new creation is not another and different creation.

Yet it is also false to speak simply of restoration. Both views presuppose a conception of humanity which fails to take account of the constitution of humanity in relation to God (see ch. III). The symbol of Adam before the Fall refers more properly to the intention and possibility of created human existence, namely the possibility of true and full humanity in faith and complete dependence on God. The Fall means that this possibility was not in fact realized, except in Christ. That is the truth expressed in the judgment that in Christ a new humanity has appeared. But this is not another and new kind of creation; it is the reconciliation of disobedient man, therefore the establishment of created humanity as true manhood. Similarly, the truth inadequately expressed in the notion of "divinization" or "divine" humanity, is that true humanity is humanity turned wholly toward God and existing in entire dependence on him. This is thus not a substantive "supernatural life" added to the natural, nor a new divine-human being, but the one humanity

tion and extension, a building on what has been built. Yet
it is also a continually new building up in the life in faith
of each member. And while Christ is unchanging and complete, the church as the pole of human response is necessarily always changing and renewed. The new humanity is
not yet fulfilled in the church as his body. The fullness of
new life is in Christ, and the church participates in it, but it
is not in itself that fullness. The life of the church is not
the perfection of the kingdom, set in the midst and over
against the kingdom of evil. The struggle of the powers
of the new age against the powers of the old age is carried
on in the life of the church. Yet the transforming power of
Christ is truly at work in the church, making humanity
new there.

3) Thus, finally, the image of the body refers to the
reality of the church as expressive of the life of Christ, the
head. That does not mean an extension of the incarnation,
for the sin of the church has to be reckoned with, and the
duality of the church's life is not the duality (in unity) of
the two natures of Christ, divine and human. The polarity
of the church means on the one side the joining of the
community with the one God-manhood of Christ and on
the other side the tension of sin and redemption. Nevertheless, by analogy with the way in which the humanity of
Christ was the expression of the being of God in him, the
life of the church is conformed (though imperfectly) to his

determined by relation to God. (In *The Dominion of Christ,* Thornton
seems to come closer to the perspective here proposed; cf. ch. I, esp. pp.
5f., 11ff.)

humanity. The witness to the revelation and redemption in Christ which took place in the body, occurs in the body of those united in him. The church is sent, as he was sent. Christ ministers in the ministry of the church, as the church shares in his sacrificial suffering for mankind and in the power of his risen life. The church is an instrument of God's action in history. It is salt, yeast, a light, a way; and its members are confessors, disciples, ministers, stewards, ambassadors, servants, slaves of God and of Christ, in whom and through whom the Spirit works by many gifts, God making his appeal to mankind. The church is not as such the self-expression of Christ, but Christ, as the head, nourishes the body and gives it life, expresses himself in it, and through it works reconciliation and redemption.

ADDITIONAL NOTE B
(see sect. 1, note 2, above)

The dangerous tendency to isolate the image of the body and to make it an almost exclusive object of attention seems to me to lie behind the insistence of some that when Paul describes the church as the body of Christ, he is not employing an image or a figure, but using the term "really" and "ontologically." Or, more precisely, it is said that the phrase is not a metaphor, but a "literal" description. Thus E. L. Mascall in *Christ, the Christian and the Church*, pp. 112, 161: "while it contains of course a certain element of metaphor, the description of the Church as the Body of Christ is to be taken ontologically and realistically"; and "it is not a mere metaphor, but the literal truth, that the Church is the Body of Christ." More bluntly still, J. A. T. Robinson (*The Body*, p. 51) argues that

Paul's use of "the analogy of the human body to elucidate his teaching that Christians form Christ's body" holds because Christians "are in literal fact the risen organism of Christ's person in all its concrete reality . . . to say that the Church is the body of Christ is no more of a metaphor than to say that the flesh of the incarnate Jesus or the bread of the Eucharist is the body of Christ. None of them is 'like' his body (Paul never says this): each of them *is* the body of Christ, in that each is the physical complement and extension of the one and the same Person and Life. . . . It is almost impossible to exaggerate the materialism and crudity of Paul's doctrine of the Church as literally now the resurrection *body* of Christ."

A full consideration of the argument that the image is to be taken "literally" can be given, of course, only in the form of a total perspective on the idea of the body, and thus of our entire view of the church. But several preliminary comments may help to clarify the problem. First, we have to avoid simple linguistic confusion. When, for example, it is said that the term "the body of Christ" as applied to the church is not an image or a figure but a reality, then language is simply being misused. The phrase "body of Christ" is a term, which *qua* term is an image or a concept like any other word or term; it is language and not the object which it designates, and as such is precisely like all other New Testament descriptions of the church. One may suspect that much of the insistence that this term (in contrast to others) is to be taken "ontologically" or "realistically" is simply a confused and confusing way of saying that this is a particularly important and revealing description of the church. And that may well be true. Properly put, the question is whether various designations for the church are to be understood as similes, or metaphors, or "literal" descriptions. (And this raises the whole problem of the nature of theological or religious language in general.) Surely all of the

NT descriptions of the church are to be taken "ontologically and realistically," i.e., as statements about a reality, the church. But in saying that the "body of Christ" is a "literal" description of the church, it is affirmed that in some way the church *is* (is identical with) the risen humanity of Christ, whereas it is only *like* a building, a vine, a nation, or a bride. This is thus not a figure, or a comparison, or a metaphor, but an assertion of identity, an equation. Church = risen body of Christ.

But then it must be asked whether this insistence does not involve unprovable and misleading assumptions about St. Paul's language. In the first place, the image is not used by him uniformly and consistently, and it does not always serve the same purpose: sometimes Christ is identified with the whole (I Cor 12:12), sometimes he is the head (Eph 4:15; Col 1:18), sometimes the head is simply part of the body and dependent on the other members (I Cor 12:21), sometimes the body is dependent on Christ the head (Eph 4:16; Col 2:19). (The question of the authorship of Ephesians is unimportant for our present discussion. In any case, we have to deal with the witness of the entire NT.) Moreover, from the fact that Paul says the church "is" the body of Christ, it does not follow that this is not a metaphor. On the contrary, this is precisely the grammatical form of metaphor. In the same way, Christians are said to be God's temple (I Cor 3:16; II Cor 6:16), God's field and God's building (I Cor 3:9), an olive tree (Rom 11:17–24), and a household (Eph 2:19). All these expressions are metaphors, used to say something about the church in a way which involves comparison, and in this respect the designation "body of Christ" is no different from a host of other NT terms. It refers to a reality, it illuminates the nature of that reality in an important, even indispensable way, but it does not cease to be a metaphor (sometimes one might prefer to say an "analogy"; and in I Cor 12:12 we have more nearly a simile than a metaphor). There is no more *grammatical* reason for calling "body of Christ" a literal designation for the church than in the case of other terms such as "building" and "bride."

We may certainly grant that the notion of the body is of particular importance in the Pauline corpus and may be a singularly fruitful theological concept, but to deny that it is an image and a metaphor is to take the term improperly out of context in Paul's thought, to overlook the fluidity of his movement from one figure to another, and thus to vitiate the mutual illumination which this and other NT images have to bring to each other. It is an illegitimate and misleading shortcut to the determination of the meaning of the assertion that the church is the body of Christ. (See also E. Best, *One Body in Christ*, esp. pp. 98ff., for an excellent discussion of the "metaphorical" character of the term "body".)

Apart from the linguistic confusion, the assertion that the church is "literally" the body of Christ creates a number of other difficulties, e.g., for the NT witness to the ascension of Christ (certainly not without his body), to the sinful and eschatological nature of the church's present existence, to the redemption of the church by Christ, and to the church as the bride of Christ. More particularly, the assertion apparently presents us with a most uncomfortable alternative. Either (1) the church as the body of Christ, with all the perfection of his humanity, is an entity other than the empirical, immanent historical being of the community—a notion we have already found to be most unsatisfactory. Or, (2) this concrete and visible community, however delimited, is simply identical with the risen and perfected humanity of Christ—and we have both lost the individuality of the humanity of the risen Christ and drawn a quite unbiblical and impossible conclusion about the perfection of the historical community. (Note the implication of J. A. T. Robinson's argument, especially when he writes, *op. cit.*, p. 58, that *"The appearance on which Paul's whole faith and apostleship was founded was the revelation of the resurrection body of Christ, not as an individual, but as the Christian Community."* This crude sort of identification goes quite beyond the most exalted Roman or Anglo-Catholic identification of the empirical church with the body of Christ. Although Robinson purports to be following L. Thornton, cf. *ibid.*, pp. 51f., he preserves none of the subtlety which is involved in Thornton's concept of organism.)

It is of course at this point that the concept of the "mystical body" becomes of special importance. That notion guards against the difficulties of the second option noted above, by drawing distinctions—e.g., between the "mystical" body (the church) and the "real" body (Christ's own manhood) (cf. M. J. Scheeben, *Die Mysterien des Christentums*, Freiburg, 1951, p. 306); or between various "modes" of the body's existence, the natural mode of the earthly, crucified, resurrected and ascended body, the mode of the mystical body which is the church, and the mode of the sacramental body in the eucharist (cf. Mascall, *op. cit.*, pp. 161f.); or between the various "aspects" of the one divine-human organism of Christ, the mortal body, the risen body and the mystical body (cf. L. Thornton, *The Common Life in the Body of Christ*, ch. X, esp. pp. 298ff.).

This sort of distinction avoids some of the problems of a crude literalism, and it is able to deal with the puzzling question of the "oneness" of believers in Christ by making that union in the body a "supranatural" or "mystical" rather than a "natural" (social or physical) union—thus also it is a mysterious and supra-rational unity. But this itself raises the question of what is meant by "mystical" body—which, as the basic term in the argument, may call forth deep emotion, but is somewhat less than satisfactory as an explanatory category.

Within the context of the Roman Catholic doctrine of supernatural grace this can be made quite intelligible (cf. the remarkably clear statement in Scheeben, *op. cit.*, esp. 376ff. and
442ff., where the mystical is set in relation also to the "physical" or "dynamic" manner of the work of Christ in humanity
—Scheeben has some very suggestive things to say about the
latter). But apart from that whole conception of the supernatural and mystical realm, and of the relation of grace and
nature, the notion of "mystical body" loses much of its viabil-
ity.

Moreover, this line of thinking brings us back to the problem
of an apparent distinction between two "churchly" realities,
now posed as the question of the relation between the mystical
body and the visible historical institution. The term "body" is
taken "realistically" as referring to a real supernatural organism
or entity, which is the perfected humanity of Christ, identical
with the body which was crucified and raised from the dead,
though in a mystical mode of existence. In this we participate
as members of a simple, living unity, an organism without
division or extension, the divine interior unity of the church as
the mystical body. But then it must be asked how this interior,
or spiritual, or mystical reality is related to the exterior, empirical and institutional community. These are, as Congar puts
it, "Two realities which have each their expressions, their
exigences and their laws, and are nevertheless one Church."
(M. J. Congar, *Divided Christendom*, p. 75. In the pages immediately following, Congar presents an interesting tabulation
of contrasts between these two aspects or realities.) On the
one hand, the mystical body must not be detached from the
church, particularly through such an emphasis on the mystical
reality that the empirical becomes insignificant; nor can the
mystical body be simply identified with the visible institution,
which would make it impossible to account for sin in the

church and would reduce "mystical" to a mere figure of
speech. (Cf. Congar, *loc. cit.;* de Lubac, *op. cit.,* pp. 89ff.)
It is important to see that this whole issue, particularly as it
appears in "catholic" theology, is intimately related to the question of the bounds of the church and the possibility of salvation. The drive to retain the validity of the doctrine *extra
ecclesiam nulla salus,* yet open at least the possibility of salvation to some not in apparent relation to the visible church,
makes it necessary to keep the mystical and empirical realities
in rather loose connection. Yet the concern to emphasize at
the same time the role of the visible institution, especially the
sacraments and apostolic succession, requires that the mystical
and empirical be held firmly together.

The unity between the mystical body and the ecclesiastical
organization is sometimes explained by analogy to the human
soul and body (cf., e.g., Congar, *op. cit.,* pp. 80ff.), but this,
taken strictly, seems to suggest a kind of parallelism or radical
congruence which makes it difficult to account for the real
imperfection of the historical community, and it is often associated with a divinizing of the mystical body which makes
it no longer really the humanity of Christ (but rather "divinity" which is the soul of the humanity of the church). More
frequently, the key to the union of the mystical and the visible
is found in the sacraments, and particularly in the real presence
of Christ in the eucharist. Here, it is said, "the social body of
the Church, the *corpus christianorum,* united round its visible
pastors for the Lord's Supper, really does become the Mystical
Body of Christ; . . . Christ comes among His own, makes
Himself their Food; each one of them, thus united to Him, is
by the same token united to all those who, like Christ Himself,
receive Christ" (de Lubac, *op. cit.,* p. 107; cf. Congar, *op. cit.,*
pp. 83ff.). Now this is a suggestion not to be cast lightly aside,
but it does not seem quite adequate to the problem at hand.

Apart from the question of the nature of the sacrament itself, this argument would provide at most a tangential relation (or an intersection) of the mystical and institutional realities, and it would seem more obviously to refer to the joining of the social body of believers to the individual humanity of Christ (the "real" manhood—Scheeben—or the resurrected and ascended natural body) than to the mystical organism with which the ecclesiastical community is somehow already to be identified. Moreover, it may be asked whether the implied distinctions between natural body, sacramental body, and mystical body, do not strain the idea of body quite beyond the breaking point.

Such reflections do not, of course, constitute a definitive refutation or rejection of the conception of mystical body. But they do suggest that this term is somewhat deficient in explanatory value—and more important, they raise again the question whether it is not a mistake to begin with the insistence that Paul's phrase "body of Christ" refers to an ontological, supernatural and mystical organism, which is the risen and perfected humanity of Christ, and then to try to relate this to the immanent historical community. This is, of course, another way of posing the familiar problem of the "duality" of the church, but it seems open to the same sort of objections we had to make earlier regarding distinctions between the "real" or "true" church and the socio-historical community. Moreover, to return to the point at which we began, many of the difficulties of this way of thinking derive from an unwillingness to admit the genuinely metaphorical character of the image of the body, and thus from an implicit isolation of this NT expression from all the rest.

As a final comment on this point, we may remark on the absence of significant explanations of the doctrine of the body from the perspective of evangelical theology. In the contemporary scene, systematic explications of the concept are almost entirely restricted to the "catholic" tradition. On the "protestant" side, we have had a number of important exegetical studies, and a great deal of fervent affirmation about the centrality of the doctrine of the body (even the "mystical" body) —but, except for some of Karl Barth's suggestions, no real interpretation of what this is supposed to mean.

Chapter VI

CHRIST, WORLD, AND CHURCH

1. "EXTRA ECCLESIAM NULLA SALUS"

THE image of the body of Christ looks primarily inward in its meaning for the church. Its reference is centrally to the relation of members to the head and to each other, i.e., to the life of the Christian community as it expresses participation in Christ and in one another. But even in this, and especially as the figure of the body implies the self-expression of Christ and his reconciling work in and through the church, attention is called to a major point at which the body-metaphor needs to be filled-out and complemented in a systematic way, viz., the relation of the church to the world, i.e., to the whole of humanity. The figure of the body has much to say to us about the meaning of humanity in the church, but only indirectly does it deal with the relation between this humanity and mankind "outside" the church. That a contrast is drawn is clear, but what is the nature of this distinction, especially when it is recognized that church itself participates in the conflict between the body of life and righteousness and the body of sin and death?

The issue is posed sharply by the famous formula *extra ecclesiam nulla salus*, "outside the church, no salvation." The phrase goes back apparently to Cyprian, and has long been a staple in Christian doctrine, both catholic and evangelical—though by no means always with the same meaning. In more recent Protestant thought the maxim has found wide favor in a modified sense, as a guard against individualism, a means of expressing the essentially communal nature of life in Christ. The appropriation of the grace of Jesus Christ is never in isolation, but always within or by coming into the community of redemption. To say that I have found salvation in Jesus Christ and yet to insist that is unnecessary or unimportant for me to be in the church, is to be guilty of a contradiction in terms, or at least of a profound misunderstanding of what it means to be redeemed in Christ. The slogan thus serves the purpose of emphasizing something essential about the nature of redemption, that it (ordinarily at least) comes to us as members of a body and is creative of community. In this the maxim also stresses the divinely appointed character of the church as a sphere in which the grace of redemption in Christ is truly at work.

Now these are concerns which we certainly do not want to reject or pass by. That they are essential to Christian faith is both implicit and explicit in everything we have said so far. But the question may legitimately be asked whether the notion *extra ecclesiam nulla salus* is really valuable in conserving these interests, or whether it does not serve more to confuse and destroy than to clarify and defend. Much of the confusion centers in the meaning of "salvation." I think it is fair to say that in the traditional usage of this slogan (and certainly still in the popular mind), salvation was defined with reference to man's eternal destiny. It meant, not exclusively but determinatively, a future state of eternal blessedness. Here the issue posed by the doctrine seems clear enough. The destiny of those outside the church is eternal damnation; only within the church can there be hope of final bliss.[1] But at once the matter becomes more complicated. The precise boundaries of the church have to be drawn. The ultimate status of those "in" the church and those "outside" may have been settled, but it is not clear who are in and who are out. And even if it be possible to arrive at some kind of agreement as to which of the groups claiming to be "church" really is (or are) the church, and thus to locate the church as an identifiable social entity, the problem recurs as to what really constitutes membership in the church, and this in a twofold way. On the one hand, at least since the abandonment of the belief that post-baptismal sins are unforgivable, it concerns those who have become and may remain members of the church in accord with all the external prescriptions therefor, but whose lives seem singularly lacking in the grace of Christ and the fruits of the Spirit. But more important, the problem derives from the recurrent hope

---

[1] Precisely at this point it may be seen how the doctrine can serve, not to combat, but to intensify individualism, by putting the claim of the church essentially in terms of one's concern for his own soul. The church becomes no true community at all, but simply an instrument for individual avoidance of damnation and securing of "salvation."

that salvation may come to some at least who are not in any outward sense members of the church. This is a hope particularly strong in the modern church, partly because of the recognition of the extent to which many outside the church (and often explicitly and deliberately so) show forth the marks and fruits ordinarily associated by Christians with the mind of Christ and the work of the Spirit, and partly because of the renewed appreciation of those strains in the New Testament which speak of the work of Christ for all men. But even when Christians have been content to consign the large majority of mankind to eternal perdition, this has been an acute difficulty.

The solution to this problem has almost invariably been found in some doctrine of an invisible church, or of an invisible membership in the visible church. Indeed, it may be argued that one of the most powerful forces leading to the current popularity of the distinction between the "visible" and the "invisible" church is just the attempt to recover a "high" doctrine of the church without letting go the hope for the salvation of those not evidently a part of the historical stream of the church's life. The church is affirmed to be the divine gift for the salvation of the world, indeed the exclusive means of salvation (for salvation is in Christ, and where Christ is, there is the church). In order, then, to avoid the unpleasant implication of pride and arrogance in restricting the realm of redemption to a particular historical institution, it is affirmed that the reality outside of which no salvation can be found is after all no sociologically identifiable unit but an invisible reality.

This pattern of thinking comes in all shades and sizes, and there is no point in tracing them out here. But it is instructive to note the similarity of "Protestant" and "Catholic" approaches to the problem. In spite of the Roman Catholic Church's forthright insistence that she alone is to be identified as the one true church, it is only the uninformed who conclude that no hope can be held out for those not visibly members of the empirical institution. M. J. Congar writes, for example: "Although for us the one and only Church is the visible Catholic Church, we know that outside her visible membership there are souls who belong to Jesus Christ. There are multitudes of the baptized and countless spiritual and holy souls in other Christian communions. We believe that even among the heathen there are members of the mystical Body, predestined to eternal life. This implies no denial of the famous principle *Extra Ecclesiam, nulla salus.* Whatever meaning this or that Father or theologian in times past attached to this formula, which has often quite wrongly been made into a bugbear, it will not be denied by anyone that souls which do not visibly belong to the Church are none the less justified and saved, and hence incorporate in Christ. The church is defined as the Body of Christ: these souls therefore must belong in some fashion to the Church, for having received grace they cannot be alien to the mystical Body of the Lord." Now, how can this be so? It can be affirmed because "Christendom or the mystical Body is not coterminous with the visible reality of the Church," and this, in turn, follows from the fact that the "Church is the Body of Christ *crucified*," that Christ exercises his kingship on earth in an interior and hidden way, working under the economy of salvation by the cross—thus his "saving work reaches beyond the visible ark of salvation, the Catholic Church, and . . . the Church, too, saves to a greater extent than she rules, and secretly incorporates more members than she can claim as subjects." Furthermore, it is possible to distinguish between belonging to the body in an "effective, plenary and visible" manner, and belonging in a manner which is "imperfect, by desire, invisible and moral." This involves two central truths: "(1) Directly a soul is in any degree united to Christ it belongs by that very fact to the Church; or to put it another way, in it, by that very fact, the Church is realized, for the Church is nothing else than humanity reconciled with God in Christ. (2) The Church is not a simple thing of which one can say, as of an individual substance, that it is entirely present or entirely absent." [2]

Though Congar may go further than many Roman theologians in drawing the distinction between the mystical body and the visible reality, the notion of an invisible membership (e.g., through "baptism by desire") is typical. And it is apparent that this plays precisely the same role with respect to the question of salvation outside the church that the distinction visible-invisible church often plays in Protestant thought—and this in spite of the fact that the

---

[2] M. J. Congar, *Divided Christendom*, pp. 222–226. Note that it is only individuals, not communities, outside the church which are said to be incorporated into Christ in this way.

Roman church so vigorously rejects the latter distinction. Both notions represent the conviction that membership in the church, which is the exclusive vehicle of salvation, cannot be limited to explicit participation in the visible fellowship of the historical community.

But as soon as this is said, the question cannot be avoided whether the prime significance and function of the doctrine *extra ecclesiam nulla salus* has not in fact been given up. As long as the term *ecclesia* refers to the visible and identifiable community, the maxim has a clear and definite meaning. But when membership in the *ecclesia* is defined as belonging to an invisible body, whose bounds are not coterminous with the empirical reality, or as an invisible way of belonging to the mystical body, then the attempt to define the boundaries of the church in any practical way has really been abandoned. Now that is not necessarily to be regretted, as we shall see presently. But the maxim is an explicit affirmation that the boundaries of the church are of decisive importance, and when it is allowed that the limits can only be defined in principle and without explicit relation to the historical community, the formula would seem to be devoid of any possibility of concrete application.[3]

---

[3] Of course, it is still possible to hold that outside the bounds of the visible community, salvation is at best a very risky business. Outside this church there is at most the *hope* of salvation, while within the church is the assurance of salvation. Thus in order to be sure, one will always want to belong to the visible church, and the "believing" non-Christian will naturally (when he comes to see the truth of the church's claim) seek to be baptized into explicit membership. Variations on this theme can be found in a number of Roman Catholic manuals and catechisms,

More important, however, this line of thinking, even when it does not openly define the true church as an invisible church, really abandons the essential nature of the church as an historical community of response in faith to the act of God in Jesus Christ. When, for example, it is said that "a Moslem or a pagan who is justified by God is, to that extent, no longer an unbeliever, even though he does not formulate his faith nor express it externally; he is a member of Jesus Christ whose soul is vitalized by supernatural faith and charity," [4] the relevant question is: in what way is this faith the same as the confession of faith in the Jesus of Nazareth who was crucified and rose from the dead? The notion of faith has been effectively evacuated of its fundamental and direct reference to the incarnate Lord in history; the unity and continuity of the community is no longer a matter of immanent historical reality but only of immediate or "vertical" relation to God; and thus ultimately the significance of the humanity of Christ in the incarnation is partially given up.[5] Or else, a way must

---

and need not be traced out here. It is apparent that this involves the same sort of attenuation of the doctrine *extra ecclesiam nulla salus* as that described above. Moreover, this argument represents the crassest sort of individualistic appeal to self-interest. Its superficiality as a justification for membership in the church is matched only by the artificiality of the kind of community which it implies.

[4] Congar, *op. cit.*, p. 222n.

[5] The point of this objection is certainly *not* to deny the universal Lordship of Christ and working of the Spirit. That must certainly be affirmed, and the problem with which (e.g.) Congar is concerned is a real problem (see below, esp. sects. 2 and 4). My objection is rather to an attempt either to make the church identical with the activity of Christ and the Spirit or to define the response of faith in such minimal and ambiguous terms as to have no discernable relation to

be found to avoid these consequences by showing how this (presumably) larger community of the body of Christ, which is the sphere of redemption, is somehow really one with the historically visible people of Christ.

If we ask, now, what lies at the root of such difficulties as these, an at least partial answer is clear. It is to be found in the assumption, noted earlier, that the question of salvation is primarily a question of future and ultimate destiny of the individual. This is not so much a matter of formal definition of salvation in terms simply of future blessedness or damnation, but of a pervasive and debilitating preoccupation with this aspect of redemption, a preoccupation which, if not the cause, is at least a key ingredient in the usual interpretation of *extra ecclesiam nulla salus*. And when such a narrowing of interest is combined with the judgment that the church is the sphere of redemption in Christ, we are led, if we are not to make the maxim a club for threatening non-Christians with consignment to hell, to find some means of extending the bounds of the church beyond the confines of the visible community.

It should be quite clear that the New Testament does not share this sort of preoccupation (with the possible exception of the Apocalypse, for which there are obvious reasons). Christ and the church are never made merely or primarily instrumental to a future state of human existence. The work of Christ is throughout a whole, embrac-

---

the faith of the historic community. And it is, I think, precisely an improper and self-defensive use of the doctrine *extra ecclesiam nulla salus* which leads in those directions.

ing present and future alike. It is not simply the opening
of the gates of eternal life, but it is a restoration, reconciling and healing (as the term *salus* properly indicates)
which is here and now effective in the church. It is new
life and present participation in the powers of the age to
come. This is, of course, not without reference to a fellowship with God in Christ which goes beyond the grave. It
is the hope of resurrection; the life we now have is a life
yet to be fulfilled. But this is a fulfillment of that which is
already at work. The distinction between the present and
the future state is not the crucial distinction. The emphasis
is always on the newness of humanity *in Christ*. The reference of salvation is not centrally to a future condition of
bliss, but rather to Christ. Redemption means simply being
in Christ.

Moreover, from the point of view of the New Testament, the community which has its being in Christ is the
visible social reality, the church. Being in Christ always
means being in the historical community of faith, whose
memory and expectation center explicitly in him, and
whose members are united with one another in bonds of
personal relationship through which his redeeming power
is at work. Now in one sense this means that the slogan
"no salvation outside the church" is valid. The New Testament certainly knows no other salvation than that which is
in Jesus Christ, for salvation means to be in him. To this
the church is bound. It cannot recognize redemption apart
from the life of the community, because it knows redemption only as that wholeness and newness of life which is

given in the community. In this sense the slogan is simply tautological, the confession of faith by the church that here in fact salvation is to be found. But if we are really willing to give up preoccupation with future reward and punishment, to hope in God and to allow him to dispose, to quit worrying about counting the saved and the lost, then the question of fixing the precise bounds of the church *can no longer be of ultimate interest.* And we have to ask whether the slogan really expresses the faith of the church in a useful and proper way, or whether it is not an essentially self-defensive way of emphasizing the importance of the church, an abandonment of the joy of new found life for speculation about who does and does not possess it, a transformation of the positive affirmation of faith into a negative principle of judgment, and thereby a misconstruction of the whole relation of the church and the world.

2. CHRIST, THE LORD OF THE WORLD

Further light may be shed on the problem if we begin, not at once with the question of the church and the world, or church and non-church, but with the relation of Christ and the world. Indeed, one of the prime difficulties we have encountered may result from too easy assumptions about the distinction between "church" and "world" [1]—in particular, the supposition that the relation of Christ to the church can be determined apart from his relation to the

---

[1] Cf. Gustav Wingren, "Welt und Kirche unter Christus, dem Herrn," *Kerygma und Dogma,* III/1 (Jan., 1957), pp. 53ff., for a most illuminating discussion of this point and of the whole subject of this chapter.

whole of mankind, or that the line runs simply from Christ to the church and thence to the world, thus that the relation of Christ to the world may be wholly understood in terms of his relation to the church, and even that the absolute dependence of the church on Christ implies his dependence on the church in the exercise of his saving lordship (and thus the restriction of his lordship to the church).

But this is not the way the New Testament speaks. The assertion that "there is salvation in no one else" than Jesus Christ, "for there is no other name under heaven given among men by which we must be saved" (Acts 4:12), and the cry of the heavenly multitude that "salvation belongs to our God who sits upon the throne, and to the Lamb" (Rev 7:10), cannot be considered apart from the context of the recognition that God is not merely the God of the church, but of the whole creation. The redemption of the world is offered only through the gospel, but it is offered to a world of which God is already Creator and Lord. The church is not the only form in which God's rule is exercised; he is Lord over all societies and all forms (e.g., the state). Moreover, this lordship of the whole world is not something apart from Christ,[2] but in him. The dominion of God over the world is the dominion of the same God who was in Jesus Christ, and whose work is not to be

---

[2] And specifically not a sphere of judgment, a "hidden" and wrathful lordship of God which is to be contrasted with and exists apart from his reconciling work in Christ. Such a notion does the worst sort of violence to a proper understanding of the Trinity, as I have tried to show in *In This Name*, esp. pp. 72ff. The entire argument in that volume regarding the *opera trinitatis ad extra* is relevant to this point, cf. pp. 192ff., 221ff.

parceled out among his modes of being as Father, Son, and Holy Spirit, but whose work is indivisible. It is the one lordship of God which is exercised in the incarnate being of Jesus Christ.

The dominion of Christ over the whole world is expressed in manifold ways in the New Testament. It is affirmed to go back to the very beginning: through the Word, who became flesh and dwelt among us, were all things made, "and without him was not anything made that was made" (Jn 1:3, 10). The same Son, by whom God has spoken in these last days, is he through whom God created the world and who upholds the universe by his word of power (Heb 1:2, 3). All things, "in heaven and on earth, visible and invisible, whether thrones or dominions or principalities or authorities," were created "in him," "through him," and "for him"; "he is before all things, and in him all things hold together" (Col 1:16, 17). Further, the action of God in the incarnation is a coming to the whole world. The being of Jesus Christ is a sending and giving from God's love for the *world*, that the world might be saved through him (Jn 3:16, 18). His purpose is to unite all things in himself (Eph 1:10). Christ takes to himself the humanity which belongs to all men, and in his living and dying makes the suffering and need of all mankind his own. Moreover, the whole world is in fact changed by the event of his incarnation, crucifixion and resurrection. It is affirmed that in Christ "all the fullness of God pleased to dwell, and through him to reconcile to himself all things, whether on earth or in heaven" (Col 1:19–20), that in Christ God was reconciling *the world* to himself (II Cor 5:19; cf. Rom 5:18). In Christ the enemy has been defeated; in the decisive struggle of the wilderness and the cross, the victory has been won and Christ is declared by the resurrection to be Lord over all the powers. Thus he is also the judge before whom all the nations will be gathered (cf. II Cor 5:10; Mt 25:31f.).

It is of particular significance in this connection that often in the New Testament the line is drawn directly from Christ's resurrection to the world, and not to the church, or by way of the church to the world. Paul writes that because Christ became obedient to death on a cross "God has highly exalted him and bestowed on him the name which is above every name, that at the name of Jesus every knee should bow, in heaven and on earth and under the earth, and every tongue confess that Jesus Christ is Lord, to the glory of God the Father" (Phil 2:8–11). And in Ephesians the description of the working of God's great might, "which he accomplished in Christ when he raised him from the dead and made him sit at his right hand in the heavenly places, . . ." is followed first by the affirmation that he has "put all things under his feet," and then by reference to his headship over all things "for" or "to" the church—i.e., not simply headship of the church, nor through the church (Eph 1:19ff. cf. also Heb 1:1–3; 2:8; 10:12f.). Also, in varying ways it is asserted directly that Christ is Lord of all the world—and apparently in both senses of the term "world," whether considered as this present (and evil) world which he has overcome, or as the whole of creation. All authority in heaven and earth has been given to him (Mt 28:18); everything is put in subjection under his feet and nothing left outside his control (Heb 2:8); he is already "ruler of the kings on earth," "Lord of Lords and King of Kings" (Rev 1:5; 17:14); he has power over all mankind (Jn 17:2); and angels, authorities and powers are subject to him (I Peter 3:22). In short, the lordship of Christ, and the reconciliation accomplished in him, has reference not only to the church, but to the whole world.

3. CHURCH AND WORLD

The picture which the New Testament presents of the lordship of Christ over the world is not a clear and simple one, and we must beware of the attempt to reduce the variety of New Testament affirmations to a uniform and unambiguous pattern.[1] That would be both unprofitable and unedifying speculation, and would betray a misunderstanding of the nature of the New Testament witness. But it is evident at least that the lordship of Christ is not to be simply equated with his headship of the church. It involves rather a dialectic which must be preserved in our understanding of church and world: Christ *is* Lord of all, and the salvation of the world *is* accomplished, yet men

---

[1] E.g., the powers are already conquered by the Lord (Heb 2:8; I Peter 3:22) yet will be conquered only at the final parousia (I Cor 15:28); Christ shall reign forever and ever (Rev 11:15), or will reign until all enemies are conquered and will himself be subjected to the Father (I Cor 15:24–28). There is also the puzzling concept of the redemption of the whole creation (Rom 8:19–25).

are called to accept the gospel; all men are children of God, yet their existence as God's children is fulfilled only in relationship to Christ; all are reconciled to God in Christ and a supreme destiny is given to all, yet that destiny is to be attained through conditions laid down in the gospel; Christ comes to all men and takes them all to himself, yet insists that "the gate is narrow and the way is hard, that leads to life, and those who find it are few" (Mt 7:14).[2]

In view of this dialectic, the church may best be described, not as, in itself, the realm of redemption or of the reign of Christ, but as the sphere of acknowledgment of reconciliation and acceptance of Christ's lordship. For while he is already king, he is not everywhere recognized as rightful ruler, and his rebellious subjects are many. As Hebrews puts it, though all things are put in subjection to him, and nothing left outside his control, yet "as it is, we do not . . . see everything in subjection to him" (Heb 2:8). The church is the community of faith and obedience, which comes into being in response to the historical work of Jesus Christ, as the circle in which his rule is known and confessed. His lordship is exercised in such a way that a church is formed around him, his Word calls forth an answering word, his forgiveness the confession of sins, his incorporation of mankind into himself the willingness to live in him; and in dependence on him and subjection to him as the head, the community receives new life from him and grows up into him. And once again, it is the church as immanent historical community, as visible church, as *con-*

[2] Cf. L. Thornton, *The Dominion of Christ*, pp. 10ff.

gregatio as well as *convocatio,* as the people whose time is the time of response and responsibility to the Word given in Jesus Christ, which is so distinguished from the world.

But when the church confesses that her Lord is not hers only but the Lord of the world, she is bound to take her stand not simply over against the world, as distinct from the world, as not "of" the world, but also always *with* the world and *in* the world. This acknowledgment finds expression in at least five ways. 1) The church stands in and with the world as the object of God's gracious act in Jesus Christ. The life of the church points to an act of calling, a decision and determination which applies not alone to the members of this community, but to the whole of humanity and every individual within the whole. The election and covenant which she acknowledges is not something she can hide away as her own private possession.

2) The church affirms her unity with mankind as the arena in which the struggle for the acknowledgment of the sovereignty of Christ is still being waged. Though the church participates in the fullness of victory and life which is in Christ, is given the first fruits of the Spirit and the earnest of that which is to come, and has already begun to live in the New Age, she has no illusions as to her freedom from sin. The final "end" is not yet. It is still possible for the church to revert to sin, and the possibility is continually actualized. Indeed, the church is the realm in which evil is most subtly at work, and the warfare against the powers of the old age decisively carried on. Therefore the church waits with the world in hope, longs with the

world (even with the whole of nature, so Rom 8:19–25) for the final word of God's gracious judgment in Christ.

3) The church stands in and with the world as she receives the judgment and grace of Christ through the world. In her weakness and unfaithfulness to her Lord, she is shamed by the strength and loyalty of others to their lords. In her self-concern and self-defensiveness, she is chagrined by the compassion and self-sacrifice of those who confess not her Master. She knows that in her giving or refusing to the least of men, she gives or refuses to Christ (Mt 25:40). The compassionate neighbor, who is without the household of Israel yet binds up our wounds and sets us on our way, is one in whom Christ proclaims himself to be the Great Samaritan and thus one in whom Christ comes to us in judgment and grace. The church receives from the world because in the world can be met the neighbor, who is the bearer of the divine compassion.[3]

4) The church identifies herself with the world in her mission to the world. It is the business of the church to testify to Christ as the Lord of the world and of every man, not as the Lord only of the church. It is a lordship already established, not something which the church has

---

[3] Cf. Barth's insistence that we "must expect to find the witness of Jesus Christ, . . . not only in the Church, but because in the Church, in every man . . . we must obviously be prepared and ready for the fact that man, our fellow-man generally, can become our neighbor, even where we do not think we see anything of the Church, i.e., in his humanity he can remind us of the humanity of the Son of God and show mercy upon us by summoning us in that way to the praise of God." *Church Dogmatics*, I/2, p. 425; cf. pp. 416–430.

to establish, and certainly not by the establishment of the authority of the church. Rather, just because Christ already has all power and authority the apostles are sent out to make disciples of all nations (Mt 28:18-20) and the church is commanded to make known the manifold wisdom of God (Eph 3:10; cf. also Acts 10:40-43). And as the Lord identified himself with the world, so must the church identify herself. Also, of course, as Christ was without sin, so must the church avoid dissolution in the world; she does not become the sinful world. But the church is most surely preserved from becoming the world when she most fully embodies the servant-form of the incarnate Lord, as she becomes the suffering servant and bears in her body the dying of Christ for men, as she is willing to make the world's suffering her own. And the church most surely becomes the sinful world when she is afraid to spend her life and seeks to save it, becomes self-defensive and trusts only in her own strength, falls into spiritual pride which holds aloof from the world, or pride of power which seeks to control, or becomes an isolationist church (and this includes the theological isolationism or extricationism which comes from too much theological self-analysis; theology of the church, though necessary, is always dangerous). Moreover, the threat of ecclesiastical isolationism is at least double-barrelled: it may be the outright betrayal of the mission to preach the gospel to all the world, or it may be the carrying on of that mission in such a way as to deny solidarity of the Christian community with the whole of humanity, and thus to deny both the lordship of Christ over all and the validity of the pattern of his life for the life of the church.

5) The church responds to the work of God in Jesus Christ from within and on behalf of the whole world. As the church acknowledges unity with the whole of mankind as the object of God's decision in Christ, so also as the people of praise, thanksgiving, confession and petition, the church exists *for* the world. Her life before God is a life not for herself, but for the world. She lives to the world, and on behalf of the world to God. She has a representative significance as human community directed explicitly toward the one who is the ground of all community, making manifest the lordship to which all are in fact subject, living toward the Truth and Good which is the source of all truth and good. The church learns to suffer after the pattern of Christ, not simply or even primarily by being the object of the "world's" scorn and hatred—for this suffering may come to us as much from our perversity and stubbornness as from our fidelity to the gospel—but essentially by bearing the world's suffering. The prayer of the church is never for herself alone but also for the world, the hope of the church a hoping for the End which is the goal of the whole world. That is, the church lives before God as "the world brought to self-consciousness at the point of its destiny." This is no denial of the church's mission to make disciples of all nations and include all within her bounds; rather it is the foundation of that mission to all. For just as salvation and new life in Jesus Christ means

healing and true humanity, rather than the addition of something "supernatural" or "religious" to an already "complete" humanity, so the new community in the church is the unity which is the destiny of the race, and the unity of the church is incomplete apart from the reuniting of all mankind. The church seeks to include the whole world because, as the sphere of acknowledgment of Christ's lordship over all, she is herself incomplete and imperfect apart from the restoration of the whole.

4. CHURCH AND KINGDOM

What has been said about the lordship of Christ, and the being and function of the church in relation to the world, can be further clarified in terms of the church and the kingdom of God.

1) The kingdom is present in the church, but the church is not the kingdom. As we have said earlier, the church is never in itself simply to be identified with the realm and rule of God, but is the human community of response to that rule in Jesus Christ. In Christ, the kingdom has already broken into history in fullness and perfection, and its powers are now at work in the church in the confession of the Lordship of God in Christ. But the time of the church is the time of struggle of the powers of the new age against the powers of the old, the time of expectation. The life of the church is a life explicitly directed toward the End, which is the End not only for the church but for the "world," when by the light of the glory of God and the lamp of the Lord, all nations shall walk, and the kings of

the earth shall bring their glory into the city (Rev 21:24; cf. 11:15; 12:10). It is the time of witnessing to the rule of God which now is and which in the Last Day will be acknowledged by all, when every knee shall bow and "every tongue confess that Jesus Christ is Lord, to the glory of God the Father" (Phil 2:10f.). Whether this means that in the final coming of the kingdom, the church will come to an end or everything will be the church, is a question usually misformulated and therefore fruitless. Insofar as the church is the realm of the acknowledgment of the rule of God in Christ, all will be in the church. Certainly the participation in Christ, the *koinonia* of the Spirit, the life of love, joy and peace, of adoration and praise, which now find expression in the church, belong also and supremely to existence in the kingdom. But insofar as the church is defined in reference to the present struggle, to the contrast between acknowledgment and denial of the rule of God, it will cease to be. But both church and world exist now in relation to the End, which is no mere ecclesiastical end, but an end for the whole.[1]

---

[1] The question of the "destiny" of the church in relation to the kingdom is usually miscast because of the attempt to start with the present existence of the church (especially in "contrast" to the "world") as the standard of judgment and then move to the kingdom. The proper order, as is clear in *Revelation*, is precisely opposite. The ultimate reality is not "church" or "world," but the kingdom, for which the church (with the world) exists. We must begin with the kingdom as the final consummation and fulfillment, then move back to the church in relation to this. Here hope is the decisive determinant, and the hope of the church is not for itself but for the final coming of the kingdom. Just because of the character of its hope, the church is relativized in relation to the End, in which all things are made new. The church on earth hopes

2) The lordship of the kingdom is the lordship of God in Jesus Christ and not the rule of the church. This means that the work of the church is never to be confused with the work of Christ, nor loyalty to the church with loyalty to the kingdom of God. Just because in the church devotion to God is expressed, and Christ works in the church, the work and being of the church is never the ultimate activity and being. The church is always "for a purpose," and the final end of its being is always God and his kingdom. Simply to identify the interests, rule and "ends" of the church with the ultimate is to make the same sort of confusion that substitutes the Bible for the God who speaks or that in a "Jesus-olatry" makes Jesus God, to the exclusion of the Son's unity with and distinction from the Father and the Holy Spirit. To confuse the rule of God in Christ with the rule of the church is to invert the proper order, to make Christ belong to the church and depend

---

for its dissolution, precisely because in that event the hope of the church, and the life of love, joy and peace now present in it, are fulfilled.

The same error often appears in concepts of the "church triumphant." If we are to make use of this term, we have to recognize fully the "distance" between "church triumphant" and "church on earth" or "church militant." This is precisely the distance between the kingdom and the church on earth. And that applies also to applications of the term "church triumphant" to the present "communion of the saints in heaven." This communion does not exist in the tension of the struggle against evil, nor is it determined by hope, but lives already in the fulfilled time of the kingdom, beyond the judgment and transformation which the church on earth awaits. We can speak here only of continuity in real discontinuity. (And for that reason it is quite unallowable to conceive the "church triumphant" as some kind of essence or true reality in which the "church militant" participates and by which the latter is to be defined.)

on it, rather than the church to belong to Christ and depend on him.

3) The judgment of the kingdom belongs to God in Christ and not to the church. Before his judgment seat all will be judged, as before him *all* the nations are gathered (cf. II Cor 5:10; Mt 25:31f.). To be sure, there is already a judgment present in the Word, for though the Son did not come to condemn but to save the world, the light of his presence is itself a judgment upon the darkness and the love of darkness (Jn 3:17–20; cf. 12:48). And the preaching of the gospel is itself the breaking into the present of the final judgment of the kingdom. But that judgment is not other than the gracious judgment already pronounced in Jesus Christ, and it is the judgment of God in him.[2] In other words, the task of the church is to preach the gospel to the world and to leave judgment to God; entrance into the glory of the kingdom is not determined by the church on the basis of an ecclesiastical McCarran-Walter immigration act.

This is not to suppose that the church can exist without

[2] Only in such obscure texts as Mt 19:28 (the twelve judging the twelve tribes of Israel), I Cor 6:2 (the saints to judge the world), and possibly Rev 20:4 (those to whom judgment is committed, and the reign of those beheaded for their testimony to Christ), do we find the suggestion that judgment is delegated to believers, and even here the reference is not to *present* judging. But these have to be taken also in the light of such passages as I Cor 5:12–13 ("For what have I to do with judging outsiders? . . . God judges those outside. Drive out the wicked person from among you") and I Cor. 5:5 ("you are to deliver this man to Satan for the destruction of the flesh, that his spirit may be saved in the day of the Lord Jesus"). The judgment exercised in the church (I Cor 5:3–5, 9–13; cf. II Cor 6:14) is expressly distinguished from God's final judgment.

discipline. On the contrary, the church is required to exercise internal discipline if it is to avoid dissolution in the world. Lines must be drawn; belief and unbelief are not the same, nor are righteousness and iniquity, light and darkness, and Christ has no accord with Belial (II Cor. 6:14f.). There are those who must be expelled from the church, though only in most unusual cases, if we take seriously the example of Paul (I Cor 5).[3] But it is possible for the church to exercise discipline just because it does not confuse that discipline with God's ultimate judgment.

4) In this context it is possible to deal meaningfully with the question of the bounds of the church. On the one hand, the boundaries of the church are to be drawn in terms of the visible historical community of response to Jesus Christ. The sphere of the church's existence is not identical with the realm of Christ's rule; it is rather that sphere in which the present and coming lordship of Christ is recognized as one with the lordship exercised in the historical event of his life, death and resurrection, in which adoration and hope are inseparable from the memory of the historical figure. The church is to be defined, that is, as that community whose being is formed in immanent

---

[3] It is significant that the enigmatic saying about binding and loosing (Mt 16:19; 18:18) is placed in Mt 18 in the context, on the one hand, of the problem of church discipline, and on the other, of the answer of God to prayer. Whatever meaning we derive from this difficult saying, we must certainly take it in the context of all the ways in which the NT speaks of the relations of church, world and kingdom, and not subordinate everything else to a conception of finality of church judgment which might be drawn from Mt 16:19 and 18:18 (with Jn 20:22f.) alone.

historical connection to the incarnate Person. Its life is therefore bound to the signs and symbols which give it historical continuity with that Person, though also and inseparably as a life in response to his present lordship and in expectation of final consummation (see above, ch. II). The question of the boundaries of the church is then not a question of where Christ is at work and where he is not. He works both within and without the church. And both in the church and in the world outside the church, there is inner perplexity and dialectic, tension and struggle. Properly put, the question of boundaries is a question of church and culture, or church and "Christianized civilization" or "partly," "implicitly" or "potentially" Christian civilization.

But that means, on the other hand, that this boundary can never be drawn with finality; or, to say it another way, no one way of drawing boundaries can ever be given finality. Proximate and tentative lines can and must always be drawn, but the church must ever expect to live in uncertainty over the determination of limits. And the church can be content to live in that ambiguity when it is not concerned to identify its judgments with God's ultimate judgment on human destiny, and when it recognizes the conflicting and overlapping loyalties within the community as well as without. The remembering, believing and hoping in the church have a way of becoming dim and distorted, and the struggle against unbelief and evil in the church is of one piece with the effort to bring all the world under the lordship of Christ. Within the church are all sorts of

Christians, some intensely devoted disciples, some faithful
and regular though inarticulate and inconspicuous, some
irregular, casual and undisciplined, who are on the fringe of
the church's life. And the edges of the fringe can never be
defined with finality. Like every historical movement, the
Christian community blends out at the edges, and the line
between "church" and "culture tinged with Christianity"
is a hazy one, which will inevitably be drawn differently.
To change the figure, the circle of the church may be defined in relation to the light, which is Christ, at the center.
The light shines in the darkness, but where the light ends
and the darkness begins is a question which will be given
different answers from various viewpoints. Or, again, we
may want to consider the bounds of the church in a
dynamic and "intentional" way rather than a static and
"definitional" way.

Of course, in a self-conscious community, or rather in
the community in the world which is self-conscious of the
lordship of Christ and the destiny of the world, it is necessary to draw boundaries and to identify individuals or
groups which have gone outside and can no longer be
considered members of the community. But such action,
like every action of the church, is at once sinful and justified; it is a judgment which itself is subject to the judgment
of Christ.

Now in all of this we are not saying that the church is
unimportant, or that there is no difference between being
in the church and being outside the church. Precisely the
contrary! For when we have recognized that the question

of the bounds of the church is not for us of ultimate importance and is not to be finally decided by us, only then are we free from collective self-defensiveness which hinders our preaching of the gospel of reconciliation. Then is the church able to proclaim and exhibit the power of Christ for the redemption of the world, without distracting and distorting preoccupation over the number of the redeemed, and without the prideful self-glorification which believes that every apparent sign of God's work must somehow be defined as within the "church." And the church not only witnesses to the lordship of Christ over the world, she is not only a finger pointing to Christ "out there"; she is in that acknowledgment of his reconciliation truly not "of" the world, but lifted up to participate in him. For the response of faith to God in Christ is a being grasped by the power of his new humanity, it is ontological transformation by the inward working of the Spirit, in healing, victory, sonship and true community as members of Christ and of one another. And because the church has the first fruits of the Spirit, a real foretaste of the inheritance which is to come, a genuine participation in Christ, she is able to witness to the final victory and consummation, and to draw men to Christ in her fellowship.

Chapter VII

THE COMMUNITY OF THE SPIRIT

I. CHRIST, THE SPIRIT, AND THE CHURCH

At an early point in this discussion we noted that the church appears in the Apostles' and Nicene creeds, not "alone," but in the context of faith in the Holy Spirit. This is significant, it was suggested, as indicating that the church is not "in itself" a proper object of faith in the full sense of the word. Faith can properly have only God as its object, and the church can rightly appear in the confession only and always in relation to and dependence on God the Father, Son and Holy Spirit.[1] In accordance with this, we have sought to show at length how the church is unequivocally creaturely, historical community, marked by the limitation and ambiguity of all human existence, yet at the same time wholly dependent on God precisely in that being as human community. That the reality of the church is defined by its existing in this relation, from God manward and from man Godward, has been a crucial and recurrent theme in all we have said.

But, it may be asked, does not the logic of the creedal

[1] See ch. I, sect. 1; ch. II, sect. 1.

affirmations indicate something more, which we have not so far made explicit, viz., that the church is peculiarly to be associated with the Holy Spirit? Is it mere happenstance that the church appears in the third, rather than the second or first article, of the creed? Is the church not uniquely and definitely the community of the Spirit, the temple of the Holy Spirit, and therefore more properly discussed in connection with pneumatology than with Christology? Has not Pentecost rightly been celebrated as the "birthday" of the church—not of course in the sense that the origin of the church is to be identified simply with Pentecost, but because the coming of the Spirit at Pentecost was the decisive and constitutive event in the erection of the church as worshipping and witnessing community?

Certainly there is warrant in the New Testament for associating the church with the distinctive work of the Holy Spirit. Through the Spirit come the varieties of gifts manifested in the church for the common good, gifts apportioned by the Spirit as he wills (I Cor 12). Life in this community is life in the Spirit, or by the Spirit, and marked by the fruit of the Spirit, "love, joy, peace, patience, kindness, goodness, faithfulness, gentleness, self-control" (Gal 5:22f.). It is life in truth, into which the community is led by the Spirit (Jn 16:13ff.); it is the life of children of God, who have been adopted as sons and into whose hearts God has sent the Spirit of his Son, crying "Abba! Father!" (Gal 4:6). It is the life of liberty, of freedom from the law and the bondage of sin and death (Rom 8:2; II Cor 3). And life in the Spirit is supremely the life of love, the first of the fruits of the Spirit, God's own love given to us, "poured into our hearts through the Holy Spirit," the greatest of the gifts and the prime test of the working of the Spirit (Gal 5:22; Rom 5:5; I Cor 13; I Jn 4).

To put it another way, we may refer especially to the Spirit as life-giving, as creative of community, and as sanctifying—activities peculiarly significant for the church. The coming of the Spirit into the life of man means a newness of life such that the "old man," the "flesh," must be described as dead. The transition to life in the Spirit is a passage from death to life. The working of the Spirit in the church is the creating, deepening and extending of *koinonia*. The Spirit binds believers together in love, fellowship, participation in one another, mutual sharing. By the one Spirit we are baptized into one body (I Cor 12:13). Life in the Spirit is being joined to the common life of God's people. And the Spirit works in the church as sanctifying, as making holy. Not that the children of God have attained the goal of mature manhood in Christ, or been made holy in an ultimate sense; but they have been set on their way, consecrated to the life of the kingdom, and by the Spirit given power to "walk by the Spirit" rather than by the flesh.

It would of course be a grave error to suppose that this working of the Spirit began only at Pentecost. Certainly the same Spirit's working is denoted in the Old Testament record as moving, creative power, which makes man into a living self, which "spoke by the prophets," which will gather the people of God and infuse new life into the dry

bones of Israel, which is the Spirit of judgment and righteousness, and wars against the spirits of evil and unfaithfulness, which (without ever being confused or identified
with the spirit of man) makes man able to share more fully
in the purpose and action of God. What Pentecost designates, then, is certainly not the appearance for the first time
of the Spirit or his distinctive gifts, but the endowment of
God's people with the Spirit and his gifts in a new way.
This is a new pouring out of the Spirit upon the community, a "filling" of the church with God's Spirit in a
way which fulfills and transforms all other and previous
working and presence of the Spirit, but is yet continuous
with these. And in particular, Pentecost means the empowering by the Spirit whereby the preaching of the gospel
for the first time really begins (Acts 1:8).

Yet a word of warning must be set against every attempt
to describe "distinctive" works of the Spirit in the church.
The Spirit is not to be separated from Christ, nor does the
New Testament make such separation. The Spirit which is
at work in the church is indissolubly associated with Jesus
Christ. That is true first of all with respect to the earthly
career of the incarnate Lord. The New Testament records
the life and ministry of Jesus as from beginning to end
lived under the impulsion and power of the Spirit. His conception is said to be by the Spirit; he is anointed with the
Spirit in his baptism in the Jordan, and led by the Spirit
into the wilderness. He claims that the Spirit is upon him,
teaches in the Spirit, and casts out demons by the Spirit.
In other words, his is a life wholly in the Spirit—which is

truly his Spirit, and therefore his being in the Spirit is not to be set in opposition to his person as truly God and truly man. The New Testament language about the work and presence of the Spirit *in the community* makes equally clear that this is Christ's Spirit. Not only are there the specific references to "the Spirit of the Lord" and "the Spirit of Christ" (Rom 8:9; II Cor 3:17, 18; Gal 4:6; Phil 1:19; I Peter 1:11), but this explicit identification is surrounded by a whole network of indirect and implicit indications. The truth into which the Spirit leads is the truth of Christ (and according to the Johannine writings the principal work of the Spirit is to testify to Christ, cf. I Jn 4:2f.; Jn 14:26; 15:26; 16:7f., 13ff.). The liberty of the Spirit is the freedom of those set free by Christ and belonging now to him. The witness of the Spirit that we are children of God is testimony that we are fellow heirs with Christ. And the love which is the work of the Spirit is unequivocally the love of Christ, the *agape* by which the *Holy* Spirit is known (I Cor 12–14; I Jn 4–5). Only the most narrow and short-sighted exegesis can isolate the New Testament assertions about the gifts and fruits of the Spirit from the whole context and perspective in which they are found, a context which makes it perfectly clear that these are inseparably gifts of the Father through Christ and fruits of life "in him." These are the forming of Christ in the believer. No clear distinction can be drawn between the results predicated of being "in Christ" and the results of being "in the Spirit." We are justified, sanctified, sealed, circumcized, have joy, faith, love, communion in both. To live "according to the Spirit" or "in the Spirit" is the same as to live "in Christ" (and it is from Christ that we are able to discern the true pattern of life in the Spirit). The new life wrought by the Spirit is participation in the new humanity of Christ. The new community created by the Spirit is a being brought together in Christ into the fellowship of the body, knit together in dependence on him and under his headship. And the process of sanctification is precisely a being formed according to the pattern of his humanity.

The meaning of all this is simply that the "distinctive" work of the Holy Spirit is not to be viewed as something apart from or in contrast to Jesus Christ. The Spirit does not take Christ's place, as if Pentecost represented a new and different act of God, a new instruction and illumination which goes beyond Christ, the Word. The work of the Spirit does not represent a difference in the "content" of God's action. To have the Spirit is not to have something other or more than Christ (this is the error of Montanists and Schwärmerei of all ages, and of modern immanentists of a milder, less spirited type); it is precisely to have Christ, to be in Christ, to be brought into the body which is his body, to be formed in his image, to acknowledge Christ's lordship and to bear witness to him. The coming of the Spirit does not add something to or qualify or replace the lordship of Christ in the church, but manifests and makes effective that same lordship, uniting to Christ.

To put it another way, we must reaffirm the rule *opera trinitatis ad extra indivisa sunt*. The manifold aspects of

God's activity are not to be parceled out among his modes of being. A proper trinitarianism requires us to acknowledge that God works always and indissolubly as Father, Son and Holy Spirit.[2] (And one must suspect that the lament that the Holy Spirit, and particularly the work of the Spirit in the church, has received inadequate theological attention, often springs from a trinitarianism deficient at just this point.) Therefore everything we have said about the church has in fact had in view not only the relation of the community to Jesus Christ the Son, but also to the Father and the Holy Spirit. One cannot possibly speak of the dependence of the church on Jesus Christ without at the same time understanding that our participation in him is in and through the Spirit and that our common life is a sharing in his sonship to the Father, in the household of God.

If, then, we seek to denote the distinctive work of the Holy Spirit, or his peculiar relation to the church, it must not be in terms of differences in the content of God's activity or Christian experience. The distinction is better suggested as a difference between "communion" (with God in Christ) and "possession" (by God in the Spirit), or between Christ as the objective content of revelation and the Spirit as the subjective side of the event (Barth), or between Christ as the content of the new life and the Spirit as the agent of the new life. All of these ways of speaking point in the same direction. Through the Spirit

[2] I have sought to make this point somewhat more fully in *In This Name*, cf. esp. pp. 221ff.

Christ becomes effective as redeeming reality, is present to us, and we are made members of him and enabled to bear witness. The form and content of God's revealing and reconciling activity is given in Christ, but imparted to men in the Spirit. This refers to the efficacy of the act of God's coming, the fullness of his presence to our spirits. Possession by the Spirit means being grasped by and thus participating in the event of revelation and redemption. As Holy Spirit, God works in men, enabling them to receive his gift in Christ; "the Holy Ghost works within us to make the medicine work that is applied to us from without." [3] Thus the Holy Spirit makes alive, reveals Christ to us and enables us to say Jesus is Lord, seals us in Christ, gives new birth to enter the kingdom, enables us to call God Father and pours his love into our hearts (Jn 6:63; II Cor 3:6; I Cor 2:10; 12:3; Eph 1:13; Jn 3:5; Rom 8:15f.; Gal 4:6; Rom 5:5).

From this perspective we are able to see properly the special or distinctive relation of the church to the Holy Spirit, without in any way calling into question the Christological character of the church (which means also its relation to God the Father). Indeed, the dependence of the church on Jesus Christ, its being formed around him, is re-emphasized as we remember that the Spirit in the church is the same Spirit which was in Christ, and that his life was throughout a life in the Spirit. This is not to equate the mystery of Christ's person simply with his being filled with the Spirit, or to fall into adoptionism. It is, however,

[3] Augustine, *De Civ. Dei*, XV, 6.

to acknowledge to the full the work of the Spirit as truly uniting God and man in Jesus Christ (an emphasis particularly strong in the Synoptics). That unity which we have earlier (ch. III) described in relational terms, as the movement of God to man in Christ and the constitution of Christ's person by the entire direction of his humanity toward God, is precisely a unity in the Spirit. The Holy Spirit is here empowering, effective agent and bond of union. And as already suggested (ch. V, sect. 2), it is into this unity with God that we are incorporated in Christ. The incarnation is not extended or repeated, but in his genuine humanity Jesus perfectly shows forth the same work of the Spirit in which his people share. As such is he the representative, the embodiment of Israel, the first-born of brethren, the head of the new people of God, the one into whose new humanity they are incorporated.

Pentecost, then, means that gift and indwelling whereby the same Spirit which was in Christ and which is his Spirit unites the community to him and its members to one another. The Spirit works as dynamic ground and power of that unity and holiness which the church has in Christ (see ch. V, sect 3); he is the lifegiver through whom the humanly historical community is made to be community in relation to God, and through whom humanly social togetherness is made to be *koinonia*. The Holy Spirit, as the mode of God's existence whereby he works *in* us, enabling us to receive his coming in Jesus Christ, thus forms the church after the pattern of Christ.

What we are saying here is not to be taken in a restrictive sense. This has nothing to do with an attempt to limit the work of the Spirit to the church.[4] The assertion that the church is in a special sense the community of the Holy Spirit leads rather in another direction, viz., to renewed emphasis upon the reality of the church as *responding* community, as the concretely historical people in which Christ is acknowledged and proclaimed. If the Holy Spirit is understood as the ground and sustainer of our participation in the reconciliation and new life in Christ, then to speak of the church as distinctively related to the Spirit is precisely to designate it as the people in which the lordship of Christ is acknowledged, which is formed as a people by worship directed to God in Christ, and which proclaims the *kerygma* as good news for the whole world. This is why the church belongs in the third article of the creed, rather than the first or the second. Pentecost is decisive for

[4] We can be no more concerned to circumscribe the work of the Spirit than to restrict the Lordship of Christ. Indeed, we need to say that this Spirit is the ground of all life, of all community, and of all witness to the truth, however partial and distorted these may be. Even in the community of evil, the same Spirit is at work—in warfare against evil spirits, in the sustaining of such life and community and truth as here exists, and in the condescension of divine grace which does not coerce human response but suffers in order to redeem. The Spirit of God which is everywhere at work is thus not some other Spirit, but precisely the Holy Spirit, the Spirit of the Crucified One. The question of the relation of the work of the Spirit in the "world" to his work in the church is thus twofold: on one side, it is the mystery of divine election and human response, which is a problem we cannot deal with here; on the other side, it relates to the activity of the Spirit in the historical and social process which visibly unites us to Jesus Christ, which we must seek to interpret without presuming to say that this is the only sphere or manner of the Spirit's work.

the existence of the church because through that event the community of followers of Jesus is made to be truly responding and witnessing community. The act of revelation and reconciliation, on which the church is founded, is not completed with Easter, but only with the gift of the promised Spirit (who is at the same time the Spirit of promise, see below, sect. 2, d.). Thus God in the mystery of his act calls the church to be and makes it an effectual means for his own work in the world, a community of witness, of service in love, and of hope.

2. THE SPIRIT AND HISTORICAL FORM

a. The pattern of the Spirit's working

If we have properly identified the central feature in the distinctive relation of the church to the Spirit, then much light is thrown on the nature of further inquiry into the work of the Spirit in the church. The questions to be asked are essentially questions about the *manner* of divine working in the historical existence of the church. Such questions are of course implicit at every point in a consideration of the church from a truly trinitarian perspective, but they come most explicitly into focus when we consider God's being Holy Spirit as well as Father and Son. Granting that the Spirit is the ground and possibility of our participation in the new being in Christ, and that therefore the erection and edification (*die Erbauung*—Barth) of the community is a work of the Spirit, what can we say about the mode and pattern of the Spirit's activity in the historical response of the community? What does it mean that the Spirit is "given" to the church, "poured out" upon it, brings forth fruits and gifts in the church and dwells in it?

First of all, it must be insisted that as God is one, and works always and indissolubly as Father, Son and Holy Spirit, the pattern of the Spirit's working is an incarnational pattern. This means, as we have earlier emphasized (esp. ch. III, sect. 1), that God's activity in the church can only be understood in the light of his gracious condescension in Jesus Christ, binding himself to genuine humanity, revealing and reconciling precisely in and through this concretely historical manhood. Similarly, in God's utter faithfulness to himself, he calls his people into being as genuinely human community. That is, the work of the Holy Spirit in the church is a work in and through human flesh and blood, words and acts, finite sociality and historicity, the very earthen structure of our common life. And this is crucial for our understanding of word, sacrament and ministry (see below, subsection b).

But God's freedom so to act, and his acting in this way, must not be taken to imply that he is no longer free in relation to the human persons, acts and words which he uses. And it is especially in the light of the doctrine of the Holy Spirit that this becomes most clear. God remains free precisely in his binding himself to history. To say that is not to deny the incarnational pattern of his working, but to enlarge and deepen our understanding of that pattern (and also to point to the distinction and unity between Christ and his church, which forbids us to speak simply of the church as extension of the incarnation).[1] This comes to clear expression in a variety of ways in the New Testament witness to the Spirit.

(1) The Holy Spirit remains Lord over the church. He bears witness with our spirits, but is never identified with the human spirit. Men may be said to be "possessed" by the Spirit, but the spirit is never possessed by men.[2] The Spirit is the principle and ground of our obedience, but just in this remains authority to which we are to be obedient. The Spirit is not domesticated by the church, and his authority is not given over to the church. The work and presence of the Spirit in the church is indeed expressed in concrete historical structures, but he remains Lord over those structures and his work cannot be equated with them. It is this truth which is endangered in the doctrine that the Spirit is the "soul" of the church, and in all forms of churchly defensiveness in thinking and acting. These assume that because the Holy Spirit exercises authority and power in the church, the church can exercise divine authority, or that because the Holy Spirit makes Christ known in the church through certain historical means, he can make Christ known only in those ways. Against such views, we have to say that the work of Christ in the Holy Spirit is exemplified by the tearing down of just this exclusiveness.

[1] Thus it simply will not do to relate structure and form in the church to Christ, and freedom and variety to the Holy Spirit. That is a false dichotomy which reveals both an inadequate Christology and an inadequate Pneumatology.

[2] Thus dynamistic, impersonal references to the Spirit, e.g., as poured into our hearts (Rom 5:5), are balanced by personal references in which the Spirit stands over against the human spirit (Rom 8:16).

The work of the Spirit is also a work of judgment and rejection of those who claim the Spirit, as is quite clear in the prophetic judgment upon claims to superiority for Israel and in Jesus Christ's breaking asunder of the bonds of the law. So too with the Spirit in the people of the new covenant. Just as he is free to use the church forms and structures as the means of redemption for all men, so he is free to raise up sons of Abraham from the stones, to "call up those who are not his people to reject those who are his people."

(2) The work of the Spirit is notably marked by a richness and variety not readily (if at all) to be contained or described in neat patterns and formulae. Life in the Spirit is expressed in "love, joy, peace, patience, kindness, goodness, faithfulness, gentleness, self-control" (Gal 5:22). The varieties of gifts of the Spirit include wisdom, knowledge, faith, healing, working of miracles, discrimination between spirits, tongues and interpretation of tongues (I Cor 12). The Spirit makes alive, testifies to Christ and leads into truth, is the Spirit of *agape* and *koinonia*, of faith and of hope. And in all this the Spirit apportions as he wills, freely, for the common good. This sort of variety in the working of the Spirit is paralleled by the variety exhibited in the New Testament as a whole: variety in the statements of the kerygma, in Christologies, and in conceptions and forms of the church—a variety represented especially in the differences between the Pauline, Johannine, Synoptic and other writings, but also within those groups. Here are distinguishable ways of remembering and interpreting the

one event which is the foundation of the church, ways which need to be taken together in order to encompass the fullness of the event (but which are also capable of being more or less isolated from one another and thus becoming centers of differing communities and traditions). Surely this is not mere historical happenstance, nor human distortion, but also the free and varied activity of the Holy Spirit, bringing into focus new aspects and dimensions of God's act in Christ, refreshing memory and intensifying obedience and hope, and leading the church into varied forms of the one new life in Christ.

(3) The Holy Spirit does not replace or coerce the human spirit. God's almighty work of grace, in which he condescends to meet man where he is, in incarnation and in the reality of human community, is just that omnipotence of humbling and love which does not overpower or destroy but establishes and engages the freedom of man's spirit. Obviously, we cannot here embark on a full discussion of the problem of divine activity and human response, but certainly it must be insisted that at every point we have to do with both. The Holy Spirit bears witness with our spirit (Rom 8:16). Being "filled with the Holy Spirit" (Acts 9:17; Eph 5:18) does not mean the displacement of our selves but being enabled freely to open our selves to the divine Spirit, to be responsive and obedient to him.[3] And, we may suggest, this does not negate but establishes freedom and spontaneity, hence variety, in that obedience—a free-

[3] Cf. the suggestive statement in George S. Hendry, *The Holy Spirit in Christian Theology*, ch. V.

dom thus representing both the concreteness of the Holy
Spirit's work in space and time and the historical particularity of human response.

The manner of God's presence in the church as Holy
Spirit is further illuminated as we see that this refers to the
whole life of the community. The guidance and presence
of the Spirit does refer, according to the New Testament,
to the development of structures of thought and act, of
institution and order in the church. It is also expressed in
those aspects of the community's life which are not sus-
ceptible of formalization and institutionalization. This is
particularly true, of course, in the association of the Spirit
with the more extreme manifestations such as speaking
in tongues, and it is also evident in the sort of things which
Paul lists as gifts and fruits of the Spirit. But the work of
the Spirit, the presence of Christ in the Spirit, is not simply
to be identified with these or any other special aspects of
the life of the church. This presence and work are expressed
in the whole quality and character of personal existence
in the community. That is clear when we think of *agape*,
the chief gift of the Spirit and the test of all claims to have
the Spirit, the love which ought to be controlling the whole
life of Christians, or of the *koinonia* of the Spirit, in which
the members participate in Christ and in one another as one
body. That is apparent also when we think of the total
ministry of the church, in which the pattern of Christ's
ministry is to be reflected in all ministering to each other
and to the world. And it is evident when we look to the
faith and worship of the church, and to its mission to the

world. All these aspects of the church's life exhibit crucially the working of the Spirit, God's presence in the church making effective his revelation and reconciliation. They are not confined to expression in institutional structure nor are they peculiarly individual gifts. As decisive manifestations of the new life they can be thought of only in relation to the whole being of the community. And in these areas the presence of the Spirit evidently means both his working in and through historical forms of sociality, communication and continuity, and his remaining free and lord over all forms.

b. Word, sacrament and ministry

Now we are able to see in fuller perspective the role of more or less stable structures and institutions in God's working out of his purposes in the church. This means especially the word (as scripture and as preaching in accordance with scripture), the sacraments, and the special ministry and order within the church (as distinguished from the corporate ministering to which the whole body of the church is called). Here we have to speak at once and inseparably of divine action and human response, of the gifts of grace and of patterns of communal acknowledgment and affirmation, of God's freedom in the Spirit to work through the vehicles of genuinely historical structures, and of the function of those forms in the commonality and continuity of social life.

Word, sacrament and ministry are to be understood as concretely visible, historical means through which Christ gives himself to be present to his church, as determinate patterns of common life which through the power of the Spirit are lifted up to be instruments for the realization and sustenance of new life in Christ. This is to point first and essentially to the being and work of Jesus Christ, for such forms and acts in the life of the church are genuinely means of the divine working only as they reflect, exhibit and express the form and act of the incarnate Lord. The Christian *mysterion*, which is set forth in the *mysteria* or sacraments of the church, is the mystery of God's working in history in the victory of the cross. The word given to the church to proclaim is none other than the personal Word, the *logos*, the utterance and pattern made flesh in Jesus Christ. The ministry exercised in the whole life of the church and symbolized in a special function of ministering within the church is grounded in Christ's own ministering and determined by the form of his ministry. Any attempt to concentrate exclusively or even primarily on the efficacy of sacramental rite or the doctrinally correct word or the form of the ministry as "in themselves" means of grace tends to destroy this order and justifies the spiritualist protest. For Christ remains lord over all rites, all formulations of the gospel in scripture, creed or confession, and all forms of ministry. These structures have their proper place in the church, not as forms simply established or appointed by Christ, but as means by which the essential *mysterion* of Christ's victory, the word made flesh in him, and his own ministry, are exhibited and applied to us.

In other words, the written and preached word, the

sacramental rite, and ministry in the church are means of participation in Christ, of entering into the pattern and reality of his own humanity. And, though obviously these aspects of the church's historical structure are by no means identical with each other and need to be analyzed individually, they do reflect in similar ways the very complex pattern of participation in Christ (see ch. V). Participation is not simply a "vertical" and immediate or non-historical sharing in the new life in Christ; it is also and inseparably relation to Christ through historical process. He incorporates us into his humanity not simply by the free movement of his Spirit upon our spirits in the present moment and in relation to the whole pattern of thought and life of our historical situation, but also through the immanent historical continuity of the church. It is in this latter respect that we have to speak of the peculiar place of word, sacrament and ministry in the church.

(1) This is partly because of their "institutionalization." The *kerygma*, as verbal representation of the act of God in Jesus Christ, takes the shape of authoritative tradition in "scripture," thereby becoming normative for the proclamation of the church. (Creeds, of course, have something of the same function, though in a dependent way.) The mighty act of God, centering in the crucifixion and resurrection, is also institutionally expressed in ritual acts of baptism and the eucharist. The pattern and role of institutionalization of the ministry are of course different from those of word and sacrament, for word (as scripture) and sacrament (as established rite) stand over against the community as ob-

jective signs in a way in which the ministry does not. In terms of function, ministry is instrumental to word and sacrament. To say this is not to depreciate the ministry, but only to designate its importance as peculiarly associated with the process of interpretation and reinterpretation through which word and sacrament are effective means of communication of life and meaning in the community (see ch. II, sect. 3). In the celebration of the sacraments and the proclamation of the word the ministry is essential to the whole process of interpretation and thus to continuity of life. Here the dialectic between the total ministry of the church, to which every member is called, and the ordering of a special ministry within the church is at once involved. As Christ ministers in and through the whole church, and summons all to the apostolic mission, so the process of interpretation and communication is an activity of the entire community. But the ordering of special ministries is an indispensable focus and sign of that activity, a structuring whose importance has been expressed from the beginning, not only in the pervasive New Testament concern with church order but in Jesus' calling of the twelve as an ordering of the community of his followers. In this distinctive way, ministerial order is an essential organ or means of Christ's work in the church through the Spirit— not as mediating the ministry and grace of Christ to the rest of the church, but as a structured expression of the ministry which Christ exercises continuously in the whole church.

(2) The special place of word, sacrament and ministry in the church is also dependent on their relation to the

event of the life, death and resurrection of the historical figure of Jesus Christ. The authoritative tradition, as formulated in the New Testament canon, is accepted as such just because of its fidelity to the events on which the church is founded. It is the tradition of the church, but stands over against the church and is binding on it because that record is judged to be the veritable tradition, the apostolic witness, the statement of those so close to the event as to be themselves an integral part of it, and therefore the norm for all subsequent witness. Similarly, the sacraments of baptism and the eucharist stand at the center of the worship of the church because they are rooted unquestionably in the historical life of Jesus.[4] Other supposed sacraments are essentially unhistorical and "free-floating," and because they do not have clear historical relation to the life of Jesus of Nazareth (nor do they really exhibit the event of death and resurrection) they cannot be genuine historical bonds of the historical community to its Lord and Head. The attempt to formulate an abstract definition of "sacrament," such as visible or outward means of inward and invisible grace, and then seek to enumerate the ceremonies which might fit such a definition, is grossly inadequate—and even more so the approach simply from the perspective of a "sacramental universe." Both of these kinds of thinking

---

[4] This is the central point of the assertion that these two sacraments are "instituted by Christ." Of course, there are other forms such as foot-washing which might also be said to be rooted in the historical life of Jesus Christ, but baptism and the eucharist are expressive of the central event of crucifixion and resurrection in a way in which the other forms are not.

overlook the genuinely historical character of the church.

In a way somewhat different from word and sacrament, the ministry also reflects relation through history to Jesus Christ. The continuity of the church can by no means be said to consist in continuity of ministry, for properly the church's continuity is a function of the whole body, and the organ of that continuity can be nothing less than the entire people of God. But this is symbolized and significantly represented in a continuity of ministry within the church, going back not simply to the ordering of the post-pentecostal church by Christ through the Spirit, but to the choosing of the twelve.[5]

We may say, then, that the distinctively institutional and historical character of the word (especially as written), the sacraments of baptism and holy communion, and the continuity of the ministry in association with these, is decisive for the unique place which these things have in the life of the church. Just because of their relative stability as definite forms and structures (more especially, of course, in the case of word and sacrament), and because of their historical

[5] Any doctrine of "apostolic succession," however, must be qualified by acknowledgment of the unique place of the apostles. The apostle is one who is a witness to the resurrection, commissioned by Christ himself, and is thereby included in the event of revelation in a unique way. From this derives his peculiar authority and office, which is therefore not transferable, but is an office and authority upon which all subsequent proclamation in the church is dependent.

Doctrines of ministerial "authority" must also recognize that the ministry of Christ in the church has to be expressed in the servant-form, thus "authority" exercised by the ordered ministry can only be functional and relative.

linkage to the earthly life of Jesus Christ, they can be efficacious in the continuing life of the church, genuine bonds of continuity and unity in space and time. They are, to use language suggested earlier, communal signs or symbols which play an indispensable part in the transmission of the witness and life of the community from person to person and from generation to generation—subject to and demanding continual interpretation and re-interpretation, yet in their very fixity points of reference which determine and set limits to that interpretation.[6] To change the figure, these structures may in a restricted way be likened to habit patterns in the lives of individuals, through which continuity in personal existence is expressed and maintained. And like habit forms, these corporate acts and patterns of behavior are necessary means of expression, instrumental to personal and communal life, yet they may also become hindrances precisely because of their institutionalization; they are both indispensable and ambivalent.

To point to this crucial role of word, sacrament and ministry in the church is in no sense to overlook or restrict their significance as "means of grace." Nor is this to contradict our earlier insistence on the primacy of God's own act (the act of the Father in the Son through the Spirit) in these ways of working in the community. The *mysterion* of Christ's own victory, the Word which is Christ,

---

[6] See ch. II, sect. 3. It should be quite clear that the terms "sign" and "symbol" in this context are not at all intended to suggest the doctrine that the sacraments (esp. the eucharist) are merely "memorials."

and his own ministering, remain the central realities which are expressed in sacrament, word and churchly ministry. In these acts and forms the living Christ gives himself to be present to and in his church through the Spirit, incorporating us into the power of his life.

Yet this being united to Christ has to be understood also and inseparably in relation to the continuing life of the church in history and to the fullness which is to come (of which we shall speak in a moment). That is, participation in Christ is multi-dimensional. The one Lord Jesus Christ, to whom we are thus bound, is the one who was incarnate, who now lives and who is to come. And the work of the Spirit in the church here and now is not to be divorced from his work then and there. So, for example, the witness of the church which is now made alive by the Spirit is dependent upon the apostolic witness which comes to us through the mediation of the generations of Christian history. So word, sacrament and ministry together are structures of human existence taken up by the Spirit (which is to say, given to the church) and used as means whereby the grace of God in Christ is given, the power of his new life made effectual, communicated through the historical life of the people of God. At the same time they are signs and instruments of the promise that Christ is even now newly presenting himself to his people and taking them into his new humanity.[7]

_____
[7] Here again we must emphasize that in both sacrament and word, Christ is received by faith. See ch. V, sect. 2.

c. The "marks" and the wholeness of the church

At this point, however, we must recall what was said about the work of the Spirit in the whole life of the community, and supremely in the *agape* and *koinonia* which are to be determinative of the entire realm of personal existence in the church, in worship, in the empowering to witness in which every member is to share, and in the total ministry to each other and to the world. Both the perduring structures in the church and the many and varied "individual" gifts are given just for the sake of this total life. They are instrumental to and express the more ultimate reality of the new life; that is the object and justification of their existence. This is indirectly shown, for example, where "word" and "sacraments" are held to be the essential marks of the church, in the concern that the word be "truly" preached and the sacraments be "rightly" administered. Such demands and their concrete elaboration, while they often represent misleading views of the work of the Holy Spirit, of human response and of the role of such forms and signs in communal life, nevertheless reflect the acknowledgment that ultimately at stake is the entire character of the new life in the community, as the life of thanksgiving, faith, obedience, love, and hope in Christ, which it is important to serve by sound doctrine and proper sacramental act. To put it another way, the ultimate ontological order in the Spirit, to which the historical-social pattern of the community is related, is the ontological structure of the love of God in Christ Jesus (see ch. II, sect 5).

Through this we are what we were not, and could not be, before. This is the new relationship in which we are now set, and in which we are constrained to love God and one another. And this is the central reality; all social and historical order in the church is subordinate to this ontological order and structure.

This brings more clearly into focus the problem of the "marks" of the church.[8] If we understand "marks" to mean outward and visible signs by which the church is identified and denoted, i.e., through which the new ontological order finds expression, then certainly any list of "marks" must include not only such things as the preaching of the gospel, the performance of liturgical and sacramental acts, and the ordering of ministry, but also the varying special gifts of individuals and groups to the whole, the quality of life designated as "fruit" of the Spirit, and centrally the *agape* which is manifest in the whole. Certainly we cannot say that these latter items are any less essential to the reality of the church than the former, nor that they are any less "visible" manifestations of the work of Christ through the Spirit (indeed, to many these are far clearer signs), nor that the continuing life of the community (*das Bleibende der Kirche*) exists any less in these realities than in the former. All of these aspects of the church's life represent

---

[8] The term "marks" is sometimes used also to refer to the traditional "notes" of the church—unity, holiness, catholicity and apostolicity. I use the term here with reference to attempts to fix the "essential" "marks of the true church"—e.g., as word rightly preached and sacraments rightly administered, or as word, sacrament and ministry, etc.

indissolubly ways of the working of the Spirit and forms of response to Jesus Christ in obedience and love.

The distinction to be drawn here is therefore in no sense a distinction of essential and non-essential, or of greater and lesser importance. It must rather be a distinction of function, which recognizes that certain of the distinctive features of the church's reality can be and are given a kind of permanent structure (i.e., they are institutionalized) which makes them unique vehicles of the continuity of the whole. Word, sacrament and ministry are thus distinctive forms and signs which mediate and express (in differing ways) the new being at work in the church. Because of their fixity they are peculiarly foci of Christ's presence and signs of his presence in all the life of the church, symbols of God's unfailing and unrestricted action, and instruments through which, by the inner working of the Spirit, that action is made effectual. In this sense, it must be said that these are indispensable to the life of the people of God in history, that the historical reality and continuity of this people are inseparably related to these forms which point to and express the whole reconciling purpose and activity of God.

But this means also that such "marks" of the church can never be absolutized. The Spirit remains lord over the church and the unity which he works in the people of God is also, according to the New Testament, a diversity in the forms by which people respond and obey God's word. Further, the Spirit (both within and outside the church) is always engaged in struggle with contrary spirits, the spirit

of pride, disobedience, error, bondage and fear, the father
of lies (Eph 2:2; I Jn 4:6; Rom 8:15; Jn 8:44). And this
is just as true with respect to the more structured elements
of the people's life as to the more varied and inclusive
spheres of the Spirit's working. Indeed, the sin (collective
and individual) which finds expression in churchly institutions is perhaps even more deadly. The error of absolutization is thus twofold. On the one hand, it involves a most
unscriptural sort of distinction among the ways in which
the Spirit works in history. Such a distinction would seem
to be implied in the judgment that certain features of the
church's existence are of its *esse*, others only of its *bene
esse*. On the other hand, to absolutize certain forms of
church life is to misinterpret in another way the manner
of the Spirit's presence—namely, by supposing that at this
or that clearly discernable point the Spirit has wrought in
the church a finite form and reality no longer subject to
the corruption of sin and therefore irreformable.

What I am saying is simply that the question of the
"marks" of the church is parallel to the question of the
"bounds" of the church (see ch. VI, sect. 4). We do and
must affirm that in the historical life of this people the
Spirit is effectually present in many ways, including certainly the creation of perduring forms which seem to be
indispensable to its continuing life and which, in spite of
their susceptibility to misuse and sheer formalism, do because of their stability provide means and occasions of renewal. Moreover, it must be emphasized again that we are
speaking about the visible historical community of response

to Jesus Christ in the Spirit, not about some "true" or "real"
or "invisible" church which is defined simply in terms of
divine activity and is only "somehow or other" identified
or associated with the inadequate and sinful responding
community. But it is precisely *not* given to us to make an
ultimate decision as to how much the historical structures
of the church's existence embody the work of the creative
Spirit through human means and how much they reflect
the imperfection which is present in all human institutions
until the Last Day, nor to draw a final line between the
varieties of the working of the Spirit and the diversity due
to our own rebellion and distortion. One cannot say with
finality that this or that psycho-cultural structure or this
or that change is the specific instruction of the Holy Spirit.
Therefore our judgments and decisions, made in obedience
to Christ, must always be recognized as relative and proximate decisions, themselves subject to the judgment of God,
as is the whole life of the church. Tentative decisions we
must indeed make, judgments that certain marks of freedom
and diversity in the church do seem to manifest the inspira-
tion of the Spirit and that others seem to be the work of
a contrary spirit, or that certain forms and structures seem
indispensable to the life and continuity of the community
but at the same time may become effective instruments of
other spirits than the Spirit of the Father and the Son. But
these decisions are not final judgments that here the church
exists and there it does not, nor are they the identification
of "marks" by which the presence of the Spirit in the
church can always and assuredly be recognized. They are

rather decisions to be taken in the utmost humility with respect to what we believe to be distinctive and enduring characteristics and patterns of the historical life of this responding people, and decisions which yet acknowledge that within this people as well as without the warfare against contrary spirits is being waged.[9] The real problem for the church is not one of deciding what minimum of "marks" is necessary for the existence of the church; *it is the task of allowing the Spirit to work more fully in all his ways of presence.*

d. The Spirit of promise

The point we have been making is reinforced by the recognition that the Spirit is the Spirit of promise, given to us as the *arrhabon*, the earnest, the pledge or guarantee of what is to come, the assurance of an inheritance, a final victory, which we do not yet possess but which shall at the End be ours also (cf. II Cor 1:22; 5:5; Eph 1:13f.). That is to say, the presence of the Spirit in the church refers not only to a working out of God's purposes in past and present, to a genuine embodiment of the new life in Christ in the historical life of the people, but also and especially to

[9] Thus we may be compelled to recognize that on occasion the most real and full Christian life appears to exist outside the regular structures of church life. Here, then, we shall see the work of the Spirit in judgment upon the church. At the same time, we may be able to see how that life has come into being not without relation to the historic existence of the total Christian community and how that life can continue only as it is brought into living relation with the forms through which historical continuity with Jesus Christ is expressed.

the fulfillment which is not yet. The Spirit leads the church to face forward, points to what God will do as the completion and perfection of what he has already done. In witnessing to Christ, the Holy Spirit enables us not simply to believe in the victory already won in Christ but also to look in hope to the victory which is to come.[10]

This is not something additional to or beside other "works" of the Spirit. It is rather an essential determinant of all the Spirit's presence and activity, in the light of which every aspect of the work of the Spirit in the church must be viewed. The varied and "free" gifts of the Spirit are gifts in respect of particular individual and communal situations, possibilities and needs, i.e., gifts for carrying on the warfare against the unholy spirits, gifts which thus look to the completion of our redemption in the resurrection from the dead. The enduring forms of the church's life are not only instruments through which Christ now exercises his lordship over the church and by the Spirit incorporates us into his risen humanity, but signs pointing to the fullness of new life in the kingdom, in which all the forms of the present will be transformed. (Thus the sacraments especially are expressions of the promise, visible symbols and seals of the faithfulness of Christ.) The communion we now have with Christ and one another, the joy, peace, love, patience, kindness, goodness, faithfulness, gentleness, self-control,

[10] It is not without significance that the Spirit and the church appear in the Apostles' Creed in close connection with a transition from affirmations about the saving event of the past to expressions of hope.

freedom, and the ability to call God "Father," which are now wrought in the church by the abiding of the Spirit, are foretastes of the communion, love, joy, peace and sonship of the kingdom. So too all unity and holiness which the church now has in relation to God in Jesus Christ through the Spirit are real in the End to which the church moves and in relation to which it lives. That unity and holiness is "possessed" in hope, and a hope which looks not only to the cleansing and fulfilling of the church but to the pouring out of the Spirit on all flesh, when all the kingdom of this world shall become the kingdom of our Lord and of his Christ (Rev 11:15).

To say it another way, it does not yet appear what we shall be. That the promised Spirit comes as the Spirit of promise means that all the manifestations of the presence of the Spirit are at the same time relativized by drawing us toward a final disclosure and manifestation. The kingdom is announced in the church and present in the church but the church is not the kingdom. And this must qualify everything we say about the way in which the Spirit dwells in the church. It requires an openness to ways of form and freedom in which the Spirit will move in the future of the church, ways which will manifest continuity with his working in past and present but which may involve transformation and fulfillment of the patterns and forms we now know, as he leads the church toward its final goal. The nature and task of the church, as people of God, as the body of Christ, and equally as the community of the Spirit, are existence in response to what God has done in Jesus

Christ, in acknowledgment of the One who now exercises his lordship over the world, and in the openness of waiting. Only in this wholeness of its relation to the triune God can the reality of the church be described.

Index